Your Home in the West

'Wooden is a new interesting talent'   *The Guardian*

A gutsy tragi-comic drama set in a run-down Newcastle housing estate where Jean, divorced from the violent, foul-mouthed Micky, rules over a household that teeters on the brink of disaster whenever her ex-husband bursts through the front door.

Winner of the 1990 Mobil Playwriting Competition for the Royal Exchange Theatre, Manchester, **Your Home in the West** premièred at the Royal Exchange Theatre in March 1991.

Rod Wooden was born in London, brought up in Norfolk, and has since lived mainly in the North of England. Following a number of rehearsed readings on the London fringe, his first full production was **High Brave Boy** which, together with his adaptation of Büchner's *Woyzeck*, was performed by Northern Stage at Live Theatre, Newcastle upon Tyne in February 1990. In 1991 he was awarded the Mobil Bursary to work as writer in residence at the Royal Exchange Theatre, Manchester.

Methuen New Theatrescripts series offers frontline intelligence of the most original and exciting work from the fringe:

authors in the same series

Rod Wooden

Your Home in the West

'When slaves love one another, it's not love'
Jean Genet, *The Maids*

Methuen Drama

A Methuen New Theatrescript

First published in Great Britain in 1991 by Methuen Drama,
Michelin House, 81 Fulham Road, London SW3 6RB and
distributed in the United States of America by HEB Inc.,
361 Hanover Street, Portsmouth, New Hampshire 03801.

ISBN 0-413-65760-4

A CIP catalogue record for this book is available from
The British Library.

The quote from Jean Genet's *The Maids* is used by kind
permission of Faber & Faber.

Little Darling by Woody Guthrie © 1966 Storm King Music Inc.
Words and music by Woody Guthrie assigned to Harmony
Music Ltd., 1A Farm Place, London W8 for the UK and Eire.

The illustration on the front cover is by Karen Jones from the
original poster design for the Royal Exchange Theatre,
Manchester by Hemisphere, Manchester.

Caution

All rights whatsoever in this play are strictly reserved and
application for permission to perform it in whole or in part must be
made in advance before rehearsals begin to Micheline Steinberg,
110 Frognal, London NW3 6XU.

Printed and bound in Great Britain by
Cox & Wyman Ltd, Cardiff Road, Reading

to Stephen Jeffreys

Your Home in the West was premièred at the Royal Exchange Theatre, Manchester on 28 March 1991, with the following cast:

Jean Robson *mid-30s*	Lorraine Ashbourne
Micky Robson *her ex-husband, mid-30s*	David Threlfall
Sharon *their daughter, 15*	Gillian Kearney
Michael *their son, 7*	Dale Gregson
Jeannie *Micky's mother, 60s*	Dilys Hamlett
Maurice *his brother, 30*	Derek Walmsley
Sean Grogan *Jean's boyfriend, late 20s*	Andy Serkis
Jill Maybank *schoolteacher, mid-20s*	Margo Gunn

Director Braham Murray
Designer Johanna Bryant
Lighting Robert Bryan
Sound Philip Clifford
Fights Nicholas Hall
Dialects coach Penny Dyer
Musical Arrangements Chris Monks

The play takes place on a Friday afternoon and evening in late November, 1987.

The living room of a first floor council flat in the West End of Newcastle upon Tyne. Centre stage, a worn three-seater settee. Down right, a matching armchair. In front of the settee, a coffee table. Down left, a television. Upstage, a large window. Left wall, a mirror and two doors to bedrooms (bedroom one, **Sharon** and her younger brother, up; bedroom two, **Jean** and **Sean**, down). In the corner upstage left, a third door leading to stairs and the street. All entrances and exits are made via this door unless stated otherwise. The wooden stairs (unseen) are not carpeted, and the sound of anyone going up or down them is therefore exaggerated. Right wall, two doors to kitchen (up) and bathroom (down), and a clock.

The secret knock (used by everyone except **Jill Maybank**) is two sharp knocks followed by two more. Again, any knocks at the front door (off set, foot of the stairs) will sound louder due to the uncarpeted stairs.

All characters speak with a Geordie accent except **Sean Grogan** (Southern Irish) and **Jill Maybank** (middle class Yorkshire).

Physical gesture and movement, and the distance between people, are important in this play – hence the stage directions, particularly in Acts Two and Three. These are merely suggestions, to emphasise the physicality of the piece, rather than instructions which have to be followed to the letter.

Songs

Sean Grogan's song in Act Two is *Little Darling*, written and recorded by Woody Guthrie. The words are as follows:

Who's gonna talk your future over
While I'm ramblin' in the West

At my window sad and lonely
Often do I think of thee
And I wonder little darling
If you ever think of me

You will meet with many faces
Some will tell you I'm not true
Please remember little darling
No one loves you like I do

Yes at my window sad and lonely
Often do I think of thee
And I wonder little darling
If you ever think of me

Who's gonna hold you little darling
Who's gonna hold you to their breast
Who's gonna talk your future over
While I'm ramblin' in the West

At my window sad and lonely
Often do I think of thee
And I wonder little darling
If you ever think of me

The Football Song sung by Micky and Maurice in Act Two is as follows:

We've got Mirandinha
He's not from Argentina
He's from Brazil
And he's fucking fucking brill

The tune to the song *Drowned Man Walking* sung by Sean at the start of Act Four (words included in the text) is 'Banks of Sweet Primroses' (traditional).

Act One

Blackout. Sound of gunfire. Then lights fade up to show **Jeannie** *seated at the left end of the settee, holding a remote control in front of her and staring intently at the television screen. On the coffee table is a jumble of video boxes, an empty brown ale bottle, an empty glass, and a used ashtray. The clock shows the time as a quarter to five. Outside the window, darkness.*

Gunfire continues for a few seconds after the lights have come up. **Jeannie** *flicks the control. Sound of gunfire changes to romantic music. She stares at the screen. Flicks the control. Sound of gunfire. She stares at the screen, flicks the control. Nothing happens, gunfire continues. She stares at the screen, flicks the control. Nothing happens, gunfire continues. She stares at the control and then again at the screen, flicks the control. Nothing happens, gunfire continues. She throws the control down on the table. Gunfire stops.*

Jeannie Waste of friggin time.

Picks up glass and looks at it. Empty. Puts it down. Picks up bottle, looks at it. Empty. Puts it down. Picks up control, looks at it, points it at the screen. Flicks the control. Nothing happens. Throws it on the table. Nothing happens.

Waste of time and no mistake. Better off dead than sittin here. Be better thought of. Eat this, drink that, shit this, piss that. Then sit down, watch this, go to bed.

There is a knocking at the front door.

Then get up, eat this, drink that, shit this, piss that, sit down, watch this, go to bed.

Knocking is repeated.

Waste of friggin time. Better off dead.

Knocking is repeated.

Voice of Jean (*simultaneous with knocking*) JEANNIE!

Jeannie Better off dead and no mistake.

Gets up and shuffles towards the door, exits. Sound of slow descending. Sound of door opening.

Voice of Jean Let's get in for Christ's sake.

Sound of door closing. Sound of **Jean** *ascending, followed more slowly by* **Jeannie. Jean** *enters with shopping in two plastic carrier bags. Puts bags down, looks around.*

Jean   Thought you'd got a bloke in, the time it took you to get to the door.

Jeannie (*entering and shuffling towards the settee*)   Chance would be a fine thing.

Jean (*coming down centre to warm herself in front of the fire*)   Christ it's cold. Cold enough to freeze your tits off.

Jeannie (*sitting down as before*)   Chance *would* be a fine thing.

Jean   Christ I'm sick of that town. Full of daft buggers doing their Christmas shopping already. Can't throw their money away fast enough, most of them. Nowt but push, shove. Ten deep round Fenwicks window, bairns can't even get a look in. Shops so full of stuff they look like Micky's back room. Lights flashing off and on like a friggin disco, make your skull ache just to look at them. (*Taking off one shoe and looking at it.*) Do with some of them lights down here, pitch black when you get off that bus. Nearly crippled myself just trying to get down the street. (*Putting shoe back on again.*) Kids been hoying stones at the lamps again.

Pause.

Sharon and Michael back yet?

Jeannie   Na.

Jean (*going towards the shopping*)   Been kept in again, more than likely, and she'll be waiting for him.

Jeannie   She's a good lassie.

Jean (*taking bags into the kitchen*)   She'll do.

Jeannie   Aye, she's a good lassie.

Jean (*from kitchen*)   I'll sort these out later.

Jean *returns from the kitchen with a glass and an opened bottle of brown ale. Pours some into her glass, then takes* **Jeannie***'s glass from the table and pours some into that. Gives it to* **Jeannie***, then goes to the window and peers out.*

Jean   Pitch black out there.

Jeannie   Aye, kids been hoying stones at the lamps again.

Jean *draws the curtains, then comes to sit in the armchair.*

Jean Should be back by now, even if he has been kept in.

Pause.

Jeannie Aye, she's a good lassie your Sharon. Takes after her mother does Sharon.

Jean (*ironically*) Aye, she's got the lads chasing after her already.

Jeannie Bright lassie and no mistake. Nice quiet lassie. Not like your Michael always rushing about. Can't tell what's in his head from one minute to the next.

Jean (*resigned*) Aye.

Jeannie Keeps nothing in his head for five minutes. Tell him something, gone. In one ear, out the other. Clean through. I've given up trying to make him mind. Tell him to stop doing something, just keeps right on doing it. Turns round and looks at us like I've gone off it. Just keeps right on doing it.

Pause.

Micky makes him mind though, he minds Micky.

Jean (*resigned*) Aye, he minds Micky all right.

Jeannie Aye, Micky's got a way with him all right. Puts the fear of God up him, Micky does.

Pause.

Jean There's times he gets me to such a pitch I don't know whether I'm coming or going. Have to skulldrag him to school some mornings. And then he won't stop. First chance, off. And when he does stop, he's working himself with the teachers in next to no time.

Jeannie Can't your man do anything with him?

Jean Sean? Na. Keeps right out of it does Sean.

Jeannie Same as my man used to be when Micky and Maurice were lads. Neither use nor ornament.

Pause.

Did Sharon tell you about the dead cat?

Jean No, what?

Jeannie About a week ago it were. Michael comes into my house carrying a dead cat. Sharon sees it and starts screaming blue murder. I tell him to take it out. He says no, his dad has to see it, or else he won't get his fifty pence.

Jean What fifty pence?

Jeannie That's what I said, what fifty pence. He says his dad has promised him fifty pence for every dead cat he brings back. So he puts it in the kitchen out of the way of the dog, and he stands guard over it till Micky gets back. Not a word out of him. Quietest he's been for a long time.

Jean And did Micky give it him?

Jeannie Oh aye, straightaway. I says did you kill it Michael, and he says no, he just found it. I reckon he killed it. It didn't look like it died natural to me.

Jean Jesus Christ, seven year old and he's going round killing people's cats.

Jeannie He never liked cats did Micky.

Jean That's no reason to tell the laddie to go round killing them!

Jeannie Aye, well. (*Seeking to change the subject.*) Well at least the bairns'll have a good Christmas Jean, cats or no cats.

Jean Sounds like no cats. Aye, we'll be all right I suppose.

Jeannie You'll be better off than most, what with a man working and a giro coming in.

Jean You're out of date man Jeannie, there's been no giro coming in for a twelvemonth now. Too many round here ready to snitch on you.

Jeannie You know me Jean, your business is your business.

Pause.

Aye, you'll be better off with this man than you were with Micky, even though he is me own son. Never treated you right did Micky. Never treated you right by a long chalk.

Jean You can say that again.

Jeannie Well you got a good man now with the money. He may be a drinking man, but he's a working man. And good with the money, that's the main thing.

Jean Not like Micky, eh?

Jeannie Terrible with the money Micky is, terrible. I'll be lucky if I get as much as an orange for the Christmas, I'm telling you. I know what you had to put up wi with Micky, same as what I had to put up wi with my man. Running about in fancy suits. Never anything for me or the bairns. Nothing for the Christmas, nothing. Had to tell them Santa Claus had met with an accident, fell through a hole in the ice.

Pause.

Maurice believed it. Micky didn't, he was older. But Maurice believed it. Still talks about it, Maurice does. When he's talking sensible like.

Pause.

Jean Micky still running round with daft bits of lasses is he?

Jeannie Not just running round with them Jean man. Knocking them off. In my house. Got one now stopping with us, not a day over seventeen. Little bit of a thing with a mouth on her like the Tyne Tunnel. Effing this, effing that. Never so much as a word out of her when Micky's about. But when he's out, cheeky. Very, very cheeky. Mouth on her like the Tyne Tunnel.

Pause.

Aye, he picks them and no mistake. All except you. Didn't know when he was well off there. Should have stopped with you like I told him.

Jean (*quietly*) Took his side though, didn't you Jeannie but?

Jeannie How's that like?

Jean Took his side. When we was fighting for custody of the bairns.

Jeannie How's that like?

Jean How's that like! Said the bairns could stop with you didn't you, if he got custody? Said you'd help him bring them up, leastways that's what I heard.

Jeannie Then you didn't hear the full story.

Pause.

Jean Well?

Jeannie Well what?

Jean Well let's hear the full story man.

Long pause.

Jeannie Cos I said that. Had to, didn't I? Flesh and blood is Micky after all. Didn't want to see them bairns in a home, did I? And that's what it was coming to, with you away in Middlesbrough, no one seen a hide nor hair of you for weeks. Living it up in Middlesbrough with that daft Denise, living it up the pair of you.

Pause.

I knew Micky would never look after the bairns. Told that welfare wife as much. Best off with their mother missus, I said to her, cos *he'll* never look after them, not till hell and the Tyne freeze over on the same day. Told her straight. Wrote it all down she did.

Pause.

And you got them. You came back from living it up in Middlesbrough and you . . .

Jean (*interrupting*) Living it up in Middlesbrough? In that dead and alive hole?

Jeannie (*not deterred*) You came back from living it up in Middlesbrough and you got them. Thanks to me you got them. And that's the truth, I'd swear it on the bairn's life.

Jean Town centre full of corner shops is Middlesbrough.

Pause.

Daft thing to do, I'll admit to that. Had to get away, else I'd have gone right off it. The bairns working themselves, him coming and getting them at all hours of the day and night, bringing them back at all hours, driving up outside in a flash car, bang on the door then gone, just the bairns on the doorstep. Our Sharon crying her eyes out. Driving me so far round the bend I thought I'd meet myself coming the other way. That welfare wife poking her nose in, asking questions. Demented I was. Demented.

Jeannie Aye, so you went to Middlesbrough.

Jean I knew Denise from Elswick Road, years ago. She said Middlesbrough was good for sailors. Sailors! In

Middlesbrough! Never saw any sign of the sea, let alone sailors. When we got there she said she'd got the place mixed up, said it must have been Liverpool she was thinking of.

Pause.

Hard town to work is Middlesbrough. No life, except for the Irish lads. And too many daft lasses giving it away for nowt, just like this town. That's what finished Elswick Road. Too many daft lasses on the Bigg Market, giving it away for nowt.

Jeannie Aye, it were the same when I was a lass. Always has been the same in this town.

Jean And I missed the bairns. Missed them as soon as I got down there. That's what finished us, the bairns.

Jeannie Aye well, thanks to me you got them.

Pause.

Jean So did you tell Micky the same as what you'd told the welfare woman, about me having them?

Jeannie Just because I look daft, it don't mean I *am* friggin daft. He would have killed us, flesh and blood or no flesh and blood. And not thought twice about it. Same as he'll do for anyone as gets in his way. From the highest to the lowest, anyone.

Sound of knocking at the front door.

That'll be the bairns.

Jean (*getting up*) Aye.

Jean *exits down the stairs. Sound of descending. Sound of front door opening. Sound of* **Jean**'s *and* **Sharon**'s *voices, raised but indistinct. Sound of door closing, then* **Jean** *and* **Sharon** *quickly ascending.* **Sharon** *enters, closely followed by* **Jean**. **Sharon** *appears nervous,* **Jean** *agitated.* **Sharon** *comes down centre to warm herself at the fire.* **Jean** *stands expectantly, as if awaiting further explanation.*

Jean Well?

Sharon (*facing downstage*) He's run away again. (*Turning to* **Jean**, *speaking in a rush.*) It wasn't my fault mam, honest. I wasn't there, it was only what the teacher told us.

She turns back nervously towards the fire.

Jeannie Well go on lassie.

Sharon (*facing downstage, speaking as before*) He was working himself with the teacher. She said he'd have to stay behind, so he did off. He was running across the playground and one of the dinner women saw him and chased after him. He climbed over the wall and the wife tried to catch hold of him but he got away. And the wife fell over and was screaming blue murder about how he'd broken her arm.

Pause.

That's what the teacher said. The wife's had to go to hospital.

Jean Jesus Christ.

Sharon (*turning towards* **Jean**) It wasn't Michael's fault mam, even the teacher said that. The wife fell over by herself. And she had no business trying to catch hold of him. Even the teacher said that.

Pauses, then her voice rising in agitation.

I wasn't there, I just went to meet him, it was just what the teacher told us.

Turns back to face downstage again.

And now he's gone off and it's dark and God knows what's going to happen to him.

She buries her face in her hands.

Jeannie Come here lassie.

Sharon *turns and goes to sit next to* **Jeannie** *on the settee.* **Jeannie** *cuddles* **Sharon** *against her.*

Jean So now what's to be done. He could be anywhere.

Goes to window, peers out round the curtain.

He could be anywhere out there. Pitch black.

Returns to armchair.

The wife had no business chasing after him. Stupid cow. Would have probably come straight home if it hadn't been for her.

Jeannie Aye he would that Jean, the bairn would likely have come straight home.

Jean What'd you say she'd done, broke her arm?

Sharon That's what she was shouting, so Michael's teacher said. She's gone to the General, to see what's happened.

Jean Who's gone to the General?

Sharon Michael's teacher, Miss Maybank. She's gone to see what's happened to the dinner wife. Then she said she's coming to see you.

Jean Who's coming to see me?

Sharon Miss Maybank, Michael's teacher. She's coming to see you after she's been to the hospital.

Jean What's she coming to see me for, stupid cow?

Sharon I don't know, talk about Michael I suppose.

Jean Talk about Michael? I'm sick of talking about Michael. All I ever do is talk about Michael. Welfare women, social workers, teachers, all they ever want to know about is Michael, Michael, Michael.

Gets up, starts pacing towards the window.

Let *them* try looking after the little sod, see how *they'd* get on. Always giving out advice, do this, don't do that.

Jeannie Aye, that's true right enough.

Jean Aye, and you knew what you were doing didn't you Jeannie Robson? (*Mimics.*) 'It's thanks to me you got the bairns.' (*Normal voice.*) Well thanks for nothing!

Jeannie Eee lassie, you don't know what you're saying. (*To* **Sharon**.) It's all right pet, your mam's all upset, she don't know what she's on about.

Jean *goes to speak but stops herself. Returns to armchair.*

Jean Oh I know what I'm saying all right but. I don't doubt you wanted me to have the bairns. You knew you couldn't cope with them, and you knew Micky didn't want them, he was just trying it on to spite us. You're not daft, I'll give you that, not daft by a long chalk.

Pause.

But *I* wanted them. When I came back from Middlesbrough I was all for turning over a new leaf. No more Micky. No more Elswick Road. Just me and the bairns. Heaven, it could have been, if only he'd left us alone.

Pause.

But he couldn't. Leastways he couldn't leave Michael alone. Always had to be interfering, stirring him up. First it was just against me, and then when Sean came on the scene he was stirring him up against him as well. But clever. Dead clever, I'll give him that. (*Mimics.*) 'Want to come for a ride in my car down the coast, son? Sean hasn't got a car has he?' 'Don't worry your mam and Sean about that son, they haven't got as much money as me. We'll go down town in the car and I'll get you one.' (*Normal voice.*) Do you know what he bought him last week? A baseball bat. The bairn's seven year old, what does he want with a baseball bat? Nearly put some kid's eye out with it, till I took it away from him.

Pause.

Do you know what Michael calls him? Magic daddy. Magic daddy can do anything. Magic daddy's got a big car, magic daddy's got lots of money, magic daddy's the strongest man in Newcastle, why he can even climb up walls with his bare hands and get into bad people's houses and take all their money away from them. It's a wonder magic daddy can't friggin fly.

Jeannie You can't blame a man for taking an interest in his own flesh and blood. Michael's his own flesh and blood after all.

Jean It's no use talking to you Jeannie. You're just like Micky, you've got an answer for friggin everything. Oh you'll moan on about him not giving you enough money and suchlike. But anything else and you think the sun shines out of his friggin backside. Always wiping his arse for him, so I suppose you've got to think that. Who did he run to when I'd had enough of him? Back to his mammy, back to his friggin wet nurse. Thirty-three year old and he's still living with his mother, paying no rent, getting all his meals, his washing done, bringing back little bits of lasses and knocking them off under her roof, and she says nowt. Never has said nowt, always let him have whatever he wants. Couldn't keep the father could you Jeannie, so you thought you'd have the son instead. Have a son and man all rolled into one. Well you got what you wanted. And I hope you friggin choke on it.

Sharon *sniffs, buries her head against* **Jeannie**.

Jeannie There now lassie, it's not your fault. She's just up a height over Michael.

Pause.

Never you mind, she'll come down soon enough.

Jean *gets up, goes to window, peers out.*

Jean   Pitch black out there. I wish the friggin council would do something about them lamps. They sharp get on to you when you're behind with the rent.

Sharon   It's Michael been putting them out, hoying stones at them.

Jean   And his dad's been giving him fifty pence a lamp I suppose?

Jean *begins to return to armchair. There is a knocking at the front door.*

Sharon   That'll be Michael.

Jean   Na, it's a man's knock. It'll be Sean home for his tea, and nowt ready for him.

Jean *sits down in the armchair. Meanwhile* **Sharon** *gets up and exits down the stairs. Sound of descending. Sound of front door opening.*

Sharon (*off*)   It's Sean.

Sound of door closing. Sound of **Sean** *and* **Sharon** *ascending.* **Sean** *enters, wearing an old suit caked in mud and work boots.* **Sharon** *enters behind him and resumes her seat next to* **Jeannie. Sean** *advances, strikes a dramatic pose.*

Sean   Taraaah! Home is the hero, complete with . . . (*Flourish.*) . . . the hero's wage packet, miraculously intact. Losing only an arm or two on the way, he has fought off gangs of marauding skinheads, resisted the lure of betting shops, run the gauntlet of a pack of savage wild beasts, otherwise known as alsatians, to arrive at the homestead . . . with the prize unharmed. And to which of you three fair ladies . . . (*Flourish.*) . . . is the honour due? To the . . . (*Bowing to* **Sharon**.) . . . young and beautiful? To the . . . (*Bowing to* **Jeannie**.) . . . old and wise? Or . . . (*Advancing towards* **Jean**.) . . . to the loveliest and redest of them all . . . (*Holding out wage packet towards* **Jean**.) . . . the Queen of the West End?

Jeannie (*amused*)   Queen of the West End, eee!

Jean (*taking wage packet and putting it in her pocket*)   There's no tea made. Michael's run off from school.

Sean (*turning away from her*) Well, nowt to bother. This is a Friday night in the West End of Newcastle. There'll be many a fish and chip shop taking down the steel shutters right at this very minute. And one not a half brick's throw away from here, if I remember rightly. So . . . (*Holding out his hand to* **Jean**.) . . . I'll just trot out again and brave the perils of the night.

Jean You stay right here and get them boots off, Sharon'll go for the fish and chips. (*Looking at the carpet.*) Christ, haven't I told you enough times about tramping all over the place in your work boots? Look at that carpet.

Sean (*unabashed*) You have, my love, you have. But . . . (*Looking down at his boots.*) . . . what I was thinking of doing was leaving the mud on and planting a row of potatoes on them, and then we'd never have to go out for chips again.

He looks at **Jean**, *who shows no reaction.*

OK my love, OK.

Bends down, begins unlacing his boots.

So, Michael's run off from school again huh?

Jean Uh huh. And a wife fell over and broke her arm trying to catch hold of him.

Sean Ah well, worse things happen. She could have broken her neck.

Jean It's no bleedin joke Sean, the laddie's out there on his own in the pitch black, it's no time for a laddie of seven to be out.

Sean (*taking off his boots*) Ah well, he knows his way back all right. And his stomach'll probably bring him home when he gets hungry.

Takes the boots to the top of the stairs.

Jean Make sure you leave them boots where everyone will fall over them.

Sean (*putting boots at the top of the stairs*) That's exactly what I'm doing my love, that's exactly what I'm doing. (*Coming back.*) Now, I'm for a hot bath. Any of you three lovely ladies care to join me?

Jeannie Eeee.

Sean No? Well I'll just have to scrub me own back.

He starts towards the bathroom, pauses next to **Jean** *and puts his arm around her.*

Never you mind my love, the little bugger'll be back before I'm out of the bath, you mark my words.

Sean *exits to the bathroom.*

Sharon   Mam, is it all right if I go round to Mandy's after tea?

Jean   What'd you want to go round there for?

Sharon   She's staying in to mind the bairns while her mam goes to the club. I was just going to keep her company, play records and that.

Jean   Aye, all right.

Sharon   (*gets up, goes to* **Jean**, *puts her arm round her*)   Thanks mam.

Sharon *exits to bedroom one.*

Jean   (*shouting after her*)   Back by eleven mind.

Sharon   (*closing door behind her*)   All right mam.

Sound of pop music from bedroom.

Jean   Turn that music down!

Music is turned down so that it is barely audible.

Jeannie   She's a canny lassie.

Jean   Aye.

Pause.

Jeannie   You could do a lot worse than that Sean.

Jean   Aye.

Pause.

Run out of people have you?

Jeannie   Oh Jean, Jean.

Pause.

It's no time to be bearing grudges when that little bairn is out there in the dark.

Pause.

Crying for his mammy more than likely.

Jean Killing somebody's cat more than likely.

Pause.

When's Micky coming for you?

Jeannie Round about tea time, he said. You know Micky.

Jean I know Micky.

Jeannie Don't worry lass, I won't be in your way. You carry on with your business. I'll just sit here and say nowt.

Jean (*getting up and going to the window*) There's no need to change the habit of a friggin lifetime on my account.

She peers out, then comes back downstage.

Look, I've got no quarrel with you Jeannie. I'm just sick of Micky interfering with that laddie, that's all.

Pause.

It's just the sitting here, knowing he's roaming about in that dark.

Pause.

Jeannie Want me to mind the house again next week do you, while you get your messages?

Jean Mind the house? Aye, you might as well. Cos there'll be no bairns to mind.

Jeannie Why of course there'll be bairns to mind Jean man, that Michael'll be back here any minute now, rushing about like destruction.

Jean Well if he's not his magic daddy can go looking for him in his big flash car. Make himself useful for once. It's him keeps putting all them daft ideas in the bairn's head.

Jeannie Aye, he should have stuck with you Jean instead of running round after other lasses, then there'd have been none of this carry-on. Best one for him you were Jean, best one by a long way.

Jean Best one bar one Jeannie, best one . . . (*Pointing at* **Jeannie**.) . . .bar one.

Jeannie Eee you do talk like a daft bugger sometimes Jean man.

Jean Who's going to take your place? I was with him fourteen year and I never could. Well, with him in a manner of speaking I suppose.

Pause.

Friggin impossible. There's not a woman been born that could do it.

Pause.

Or would want to. Not now.

Pause / sound of splashing from bathroom. Then sound of a large car pulling up outside. Sound of car door being slammed.

Jean Talk of the friggin devil.

Loud knocking at front door.

Jeannie Christ, good job the old feller's deaf downstairs.

Jean *exits, sound of descending. Sound of front door opening. Sound of* **Micky** *ascending, two stairs at a time. Sound of front door closing, sound of* **Jean** *ascending.* **Micky** *enters carrying a new bright yellow child's bike, which he props underneath the window. Raises a hand in greeting to* **Jeannie**, *comes down right to sit on the arm of the armchair.* **Jean** *enters, comes down left to face him.*

Jean What's the idea of that friggin bike?

Micky Take Jeannie for a ride.

Jeannie Eeee.

Micky Early present for the Christmas. Make sure the bairn goes to school. If he goes, he can ride it. If he wags off, then Santa Claus takes it back.

Jean It's too late for that now, he's run off again. And some wife's broke her arm chasing after him.

Micky How's that like?

Jean Teacher tried to keep him in, so he did off. Some dinner wife chased after him and fell over and broke her arm. And now he's off somewhere, God knows where he is.

Micky Oh aye.

Jean So we'll wait here while you go and look for him. In the car.

Micky How's that like?

Jean Christ man, the bairn's out roaming around in the dark somewhere.

Micky No he's not.

Jean How's that?

Micky He's with me.

Jean (*confused*) Where, in the car?

Micky Na, in the house. I'll bring him back later. What happened to his baseball bat?

Jean What . . . is he all right?

Micky Course he's all right. Watching tele with Maurice and Susie.

Jean (*turning away*) Jesus Christ.

Micky What happened to his baseball bat?

Jean Fuck knows.

Micky WHAT HAPPENED TO HIS FUCKING BASE-BALL BAT?

Jean I took it off him. He nearly took some bairn's eye out with it.

Micky Let's have a look at it.

Jean Jesus Christ.

Jean *exits to bedroom two, returns with a muddy baseball bat, gives it to* **Micky**.

Micky What happened to it?

Jean What'd you mean what happened to it?

Micky It's all covered in mud.

Jean He got it like that.

Micky I'm not taking it back like that.

Jean Taking it back where?

Micky To mine. Teach him how to use it properly. No use leaving it up to you.

Jean   No, I never quite got round to learning how to play baseball. Stupid of me.

Micky (*holding it out to her*) Wash it.

Jean   I'm not your friggin skivvy. Give it to her (*Indicating* **Jeannie**.) to wash. Or why not to (*Child's voice.*) 'Susie'.

Micky   Your fault it got messed up. Wash it.

Jean (*turning away*) Away and fuck yourself with it.

Micky   WASH IT.

Jean (*turning back*) JESUS CHRIST. (*Taking the bat.*) I'LL WASH IT, I'LL WASH IT, I'LL WASH IT. I HOPE (*Going into the kitchen, slamming kitchen door behind her.*) . . . I HOPE HE KILLS SOME POOR LITTLE FUCKER WITH IT.

Music increases in volume from bedroom one.

Micky   TURN THAT DOWN.

Music is abruptly turned down.

Jeannie   Eee, she's up a height and no mistake. Been up a height all afternoon.

Jean *returns with clean bat, hands it to* **Micky**.

Jean   Satisfied?

Micky   It'll do.

Jean   How come you didn't bring him straight back?

Micky   How's that like?

Jean   When he got to yours from school, how come you didn't bring him straight back here? Didn't you think I'd be worried out of my wits, wondering what'd happened to him?

Micky   Should have known he'd come to me, always does when someone's upset him.

Jean   Upset him? Upset *him*?

She turns away, trying to keep a grip on herself.

Didn't you think *I'd* be upset? What'd you think I am, a friggin block of wood?

Micky   Only from the neck up.

Gets up, begins to walk about upstage, swinging the bat.

Well, he's all right now, so nowt to bother. Watching tele with Maurice and Susie. I'll bring him back for his bed-time.

Jean So you've left him with a daft bit of a lass and mental Maurice. He could be up to owt by the time you get back. (*Mutters.*) Killed a few more cats, more than likely.

Micky (*bat on shoulder*) What's that about cats?

Jean That's what I'd like to know. Fifty pence for a dead cat by all accounts. Haven't I got enough trouble as it is without him bringing home dead cats and killing them?

Micky Wrong way round.

Jean Huh?

Micky Wrong way round. He kills them first, then brings them home.

Jean (*turning away*) Jesus Christ.

Micky Anyway, it's got nowt to do with you. Teaching him. Nowt faster than cats. Good practice . . . (*Sudden downward movement with the bat.*) . . . for the footwork. Don't worry, he won't bring them back here, he knows you've not got fifty pence. State of this room, looks like you spent your last fifty pence on a dozen rolls of wallpaper.

Pause.

Jean So who's this Susie you're knocking round with?

Micky What's it to you like?

Jean It's got a lot to do with me. She's looking after Michael.

Micky Nice lass. Smart lass. Comes from Cowgate.

Jean Hah! Cowgate! Well there's the answer anyway. There's nowt but cows come out of Cowgate. It's rightly named, Cowgate, and no mistake.

Micky Watch your lip, Jean.

Pause / they look at each other. Then bathroom door opens and **Sean** *appears, wearing a dressing gown, his hair wet.*

Sean Evenin' all.

Micky Well if it's not the singing potato from across the Irish Sea.

Sean (*bowing, then going towards bedroom two*) The very same.
Appearing at the West End Social Club for your delight tonight,
Sean Grogan, the singing potato from across the Irish Sea. Yes,
I like that, it's got a certain ring to it.

He pauses by the door of bedroom two.

Well I'm sorry I can't spend any more time with you ladies and
gentlemen, but I have a pressing engagement with a pair of
trousers.

Bows, exits to bedroom two.

Jeannie Eee, he's a cracker that Sean.

Micky (*looking at* **Jean**) You said it.

He looks at himself in the mirror.

Ho'way then Jeannie, let's take you to see your grandbairn.

Jeannie *starts to get up slowly.*

Jean D'you want to use the toilet before you go?

Jeannie Jesus Christ Jean, I'm only going as far as me own
house.

She starts towards the stairs, pauses half-way to turn and look at **Jean**.

I'll see you next week lass.

Jean Aye.

Jeannie And don't you worry about the bairn. Micky'll take
him in hand.

Jean Aye, I know.

Jeannie *shuffles to the top of the stair, exits. Sound of slow descending.*

Micky (*pointing at the bike with the bat*) Don't forget, no school, no
bike.

Jean Aye.

Micky *exits. Sound of descending.* **Jean** *stares after him for a moment.
Then seems to remember something and hurries towards the top of the
stairs. Sound of front door opening.*

Jean (*looking down the stairs*) Bring him back by seven.

Pause.

Seven, do you hear?

Sound of front door being slammed shut. **Jean** *comes back to sit on the arm of the armchair. Sound of car door being slammed, twice. Sound of car starting up and driving away. Music increases in volume from bedroom one.*

Lights fade to black.

Act Two

Lights fade up to reveal the set as at the end of Act One, except that the clock now shows seven o'clock. **Sean** *is standing left looking at himself in the mirror and fiddling with a bootlace tie. He wears a white shirt with pleats down the front, a 'cowboy' style suit, and highly polished boots. A guitar case is laying near the television.* **Jean** *is seated in the armchair, eating chips out of newspaper. The muffled sound of pop music is coming from bedroom one.*

Sean How about this one?

Pauses, then goes into his club routine.

Ladies and gentlemen, I'm afraid we have some bad news for you. We've just heard that a nuclear bomb has fallen on the West End of Newcastle. The good news is that it's only done eight pounds worth of damage.

Pause.

Well, what'd you think?

Jean I don't get it.

Sean Jesus. Look, the joke is that things are so bad in the West End of Newcastle that even if a bomb fell on it, you wouldn't notice that much difference, right?

Jean Doesn't sound like the sort of joke you should be telling at the West End Social Club. Pretty touchy about the West End, some of them in there.

Sean Well it doesn't have to be about the West End does it? Could be anywhere up here. Gateshead.

Pauses, then club routine.

Ladies and gentlemen, I'm afraid we have some bad news for you. We've just heard that a nuclear bomb has fallen on Gateshead. The good news is that it's only done eight pounds worth of damage. (*Going back to normal voice.*) Gateshead, that's OK. Not likely to be anybody there from Gateshead. Or Sunderland. Or Middlesbrough. I wonder how far South you have to go before it stops being funny?

Music is switched off. **Sharon** *emerges from bedroom one. She has changed into her 'going out' clothes.*

Sharon See you later mam.

Jean Where's my change from the fish and chips?

Sharon It was only fifty pence mam.

Jean *holds her hand out,* **Sharon** *gives it her.*

Sean (*going into his routine*) D'you know why they made the fifty pence piece that shape ladies and gentlemen? Well, it was so you'd be able to get it out of Jean Robson's hand with a spanner.

Jean (*ignoring him*) Back by eleven mind.

Sean (*suddenly realising*) Hey, where are you going?

Sharon *glances at him then exits. Sound of descending, front door slams.*

Where's she going?

Jean Round to Mandy's, help her watch the bairns.

Sean Christ man, she was supposed to be staying in so we could go to the club.

Jean You can go to the club, nowt to stop you.

Sean So *we* could go I said. So you could see my act.

Jean I see enough of that in here, no need to go to the club.

Pauses, realises she's offended him.

Look Sean man, I'll come another time right? I've got to stay in for Micky bringing back Michael anyway. And that teacher's supposed to be coming.

Sean Never known you to stay in for a teacher before.

Jean Look man, I'm staying in, all right? I just want a bit of peace and quiet that's all. Christ man, I've had Jeannie here all day telling me how many favours she's done me, then Michael runs off and breaks some wife's arm, and then Micky turns up in one of his moods, like it's God's day off and he's been left in charge of the world.

Pause.

So, I'm staying in. Just me, and the tele, and a few bottles of brown ale. Got it?

Sean Christ Jean man, I've been practising that song all week, just so you could hear it.

Jean Well I've heard it. All week.

Sean No you haven't, not all the way through. Not the way I'll be singing it at the club you haven't. Not with me patter and all that.

Pause.

Christ man, you could have asked Micky to keep the bairn till later, till tomorrow even. Then we could have all gone out. Wouldn't have done any harm for once.

Jean You haven't got a friggin clue have you? First someone's got to stay in to watch the house, else they'll be breaking in, and second, I'm not leaving Michael all night in a friggin knocking shop.

Pause.

Besides, give Micky an inch and he takes a million bleedin miles. Probably never see the bairn again.

Sean (*low voice*) Oh dear.

Jean (*trying to soften*) Look, if you want to do the song for us, do it now. Just like in the club, only here.

Sean It won't be the same.

Jean Look, I'll . . . I'll come next week for definite.

Pause.

Ho'way man.

Sean (*resigned*) OK.

Goes to guitar case, gets out guitar, sits on left end of the settee and begins tuning up.

Jean Do you have to do all that farting about?

Sean What farting about?

Jean All that plonking about, before you start.

Sean It's not just plonking about, it's called tuning up.

Jean Oh.

He finishes tuning.

Sean Right.

He starts to strum the opening chords of 'Little Darling'. There is a knocking at the front door – a stranger's knock.

Sean (*stopping*) Jesus Christ.

Jean (*going over to the window, peering out*) Can't see anyone. Must be that friggin teacher.

Sean Well, it can't be anyone we *know*, cos they haven't got . . . (*Knocking on guitar.*) . . . the special knock, have they? So it's either . . . (*Low dramatic chord.*) . . . the polis, or, it's . . . (*High chord.*) . . . a social worker, or, it's . . . (*Several chords.*) . . . a reporter from the *Evening Chronicle*, come to do a story on the new singing sensation of the West End.

Going into a rock 'n' roll routine.

Yeah the special knock, the special knock, everybody's gotta know the special knock.

Jean Give it a rest will you?

Renewed knocking at the front door.

Sean Is there anybody there, said the traveller, knocking at the moonlit door.

Jean (*going to the top of the stairs*) Who is it?

Sean *The Traveller*, Walter de la Mare.

Jill (*off, muffled*) Michael's teacher, Jill Maybank.

Jean (*simultaneously, to* **Sean**) Who are you calling a friggin mare? (*Shouting downstairs.*) Who?

Jill (*off, louder*) Jill Maybank, Michael's teacher.

Jean It's Michael's teacher.

Sean Either her or Princess Diana, I knew it had to be one of them two. Well, let the woman in then. The world waits with bated breath.

Exit **Jean**, *sound of descending.*

Sean (*strumming guitar and singing*) One of them two, I knew it had to be one of them two . . .

Stops strumming, speaks to himself.

Did my songs send out certain of those men the English shot?

Sound of door opening, sound of muffled voices, sound of door closing, sound of **Jean** *and* **Jill** *ascending.*

Sean   Oh well, probably not.

Enter **Jean**, *followed by* **Jill**.

Jean   Michael's teacher.

Jill   (*to* **Sean**)   Jill Maybank. Pleased to meet you Mr Robson.

Sean   Mr Robson? I'm sorry, but that particular honour only belongs to one man, and it's not me. You'll recognise Mr Robson by the shining light behind his head. Usually coming from a policeman's torch. (*Sings and strums.*) One Micky Robson, oh there's only one Micky Robson . . .

Jill   I'm sorry, I don't understand. You're not Mr Robson?

Sean   No, Mr Robson is no longer with us.

Jill   I'm sorry to hear that.

Sean   Yes, he's gone to higher things. He lives on top of a hill in Blakelaw.

Jean   For Christ's sake shut up man. (*Motioning towards settee.*) Sit down if you like.

Jill   (*sitting at right end of the settee*)   Thank you.

Jean   (*sitting in armchair*)   This is Sean Grogan, he lives here.

Sean   We're cohabiting.

Jean   (*under her breath*)   For Christ's sake.

Pause.

She's come to see me about Michael.

Sean   Ah.

Pause.

Jean   Well, ho'way then.

Sean   Ah.

Starts strumming beginning of song as before.

Jean   For Christ's sake, what you doing man?

Sean   You said ho'way.

Jean   I meant ho'way off out of it, not ho'way start up that daft song.

Sean You said you wanted to hear it. (*To* **Jill**.) I'm on at the club tonight. West End Social. Come down if you've got nowt on. Someone'll sign you in, no bother. (*Strums.*) I was just going to try out my song when you knocked at the door.

Jill Oh please, go ahead, don't let me interrupt you.

Pause.

I'd like to hear it.

Jean And I'm sure that Sean would just *love* to play it for you.

Sean Of course. (*To* **Jill**.) You're sure now.

Jill Oh yes, absolutely. I'd love to hear it, honestly.

Sean (*sitting on left arm of the settee*) Right then.

He strums a few chords, then sings the song, which is Woody Guthrie's 'Little Darling'. He directs it mainly towards **Jean**, *with occasional glances at* **Jill**. *Both women are initially embarrassed –* **Jill** *because of the unfamiliar situation and* **Jean** *because he is 'showing her up' – but as the song progresses their attitudes change,* **Jill** *becoming interested and* **Jean** *almost proud.*

Sean That's it.

Jill Why that's wonderful Mr Grogan. (*To* **Jean**.) You must be very proud of him.

Sean (*holding out his hand to* **Jill**) Call me Sean.

Jill (*shaking his hand*) Isn't that a Woody Guthrie song?

Sean It is. Fancy you knowing that. And all about the West End of Newcastle, did you notice?

Sean *and* **Jill** *share the joke,* **Jean** *doesn't.*

Jill I had a friend at college who played the guitar. He used to sing Woody Guthrie songs.

Sean Did he now? Did he know any Jimmy Rogers songs by any chance?

Starts playing Jimmy Rogers type chords.

Jill No, I don't think . . .

Jean (*interrupting*) That's enough Sean man.

Sean *stops dramatically, looks at her.*

Just one song, remember?

Sean I do indeed my love. My humble apologies Miss Maybank. (*Getting up.*) And that's a fine name for a frosty morning, if you don't mind me saying so. (*Putting guitar away in case.*) Well, I'll be leaving you ladies to your deliberations. (*To* **Jean**.) Any chance of a sub, my love?

Jean *sighs, puts her hand in her pocket, gives him a five pound note.*

Sean (*staring at it*) Well, I'm not going to get pissed on this, and that's for sure.

Jean That's the idea.

Pause.

Anyway, you'll be bought drinks. If they like your song.

Sean And how could they not, eh Miss Maybank? You know, my life's been ruined by just one thing: drink, women, and the horses.

Jill (*amused*) I thought you said just one thing?

Sean Aye well, I know it was definitely one of them three.

Pauses, then bows.

Well, I'll bid you ladies goodnight. See you . . . in the moon.

Sean *exits carrying guitar case. Sound of him descending, whistling. Sound of front door opening and closing. There is a few seconds pause before* **Jill** *speaks.*

Jill He seems like a nice man.

Pause.

How does he get on with Michael?

Pause / no response from **Jean**.

Look, I've not come to pry into your family business Mrs Robson. It's just that I'm worried about Michael, worried about how to handle him. And after today's incident, I . . .

Jean (*interrupting*) What about today's . . . *incident?*

Jill Has Sharon told you about it?

Jean Aye.

Jill About the dinner lady breaking her arm?

Jean She said it wasn't Michael's fault. Even according to you she said.

Jill No, it wasn't Michael's fault directly. But he *was* running away again Mrs Robson, and the headmaster has said . . .

Jean (*interrupting*) That stupid bastard.

Jill The headmaster has said that he must be suspended from school, until we . . .

Jean (*interrupting*) Suspended? Expelled you mean?

Jill It's just for the time being. Until we've talked to the Social Services.

Jean What have they got to do with it?

Jill Well, as you know, Sharon and Michael are under the care of the Social Services, and . . .

Jean (*interrupting*) Supervision.

Jill I'm sorry?

Jean Supervision. Supervision orders, not care orders. You said care.

Jill I'm sorry, I didn't mean care, it was just an expression I . . .

Jean (*interrupting*) They're under supervision from the divorce court. Since I got custody. Nothing they've done wrong.

Jill Of course not. I'm sorry, I didn't know about the divorce. I just knew they were under the . . . under the Social Services. I expect the headmaster knows.

Jean Oh he'll know all right. Even knows what colour toilet paper I use, that bloke.

Pause.

What have you got to talk to them for?

Pause, then scornfully.

Social workers.

Jill Because of Michael running away. It's . . .

Jean (*interrupting*) I've always checked him. It's not for the want of the good hidings I've given him.

Jill Well I don't think . . . (*Stops, starts again.*) . . . About the running away. It's got to at least two or three times a week now Mrs Robson. And with what's happened today, the . . .

Jean (*interrupting*) Which you said wasn't his fault.

Jill The headmaster has said we can't go on like this. We've got to find out what's upsetting him, and . . .

Jean (*interrupting*) What'd you mean, upsetting him?

Pause.

Christ.

Pause.

Jill Well it's not normal for a child of seven to keep running away from school Mrs Robson, and . . .

Jean (*getting up, walking upstage*) *Normal*, what d'you know about what's normal? Have you got any bairns?

Jill I'm not married.

Jean What's that got to do with anything? *Married*. Well I'm not *married* either, in case you didn't know.

Jill No, but you . . .

Jean (*interrupting*) No but I *was* married, is that what you were going to say? Oh I was married all right. Married in a manner of speaking I suppose.

Jill I'm sorry, I don't see quite what . . .

Jean (*interrupting*) You don't see quite what this has got to do with Michael, is that it?

Long pause.

Look, d'you want a drink? I'm having one. We've only got brown ale mind.

Jill I don't know. Well, yes, perhaps just a small one.

Jean (*going into the kitchen*) They only come in one size. You can have some of mine.

She reappears with an opened bottle of brown ale and two glasses. Pours a small amount into one glass and hands it to **Jill***, pours the rest for herself. Sits down in armchair.*

Jill Thank you.

Pause.

You were saying. About being married. To Mr Robson was it?

Jean To Micky. Mr Robson's name is Micky.

Long pause.

I was sixteen when I met him, Micky. He was the same as me,
just hanging about the streets. I'd just been hoyed out by me
ma, she reckoned I was after her fancy man. Other way round
more like. Every time she went out there he'd be, creeping up to
us, begging us to go with him. In the end I did, just for a bit of
peace and quiet. She came back, caught us at it. Called me a lot
of names I didn't understand. At the time like.

Pause.

I was glad to be out of it. Micky was different, he'd done things I
never had, been in and out of homes and the like. On the run
from one when I met him. He was the one got me working
Elswick Road. We were a team, the two of us. My job was to get
the men, lead them on. Didn't take much leading, most of them.

Pause.

And then, when they were nicely away with it, Micky would
turn up. Never caught on, most of them, too busy with the job in
hand I suppose. Till it was too late. Rob them of everything,
Micky would, not even leave them with their bus fare home. Or
their car keys, the posh ones. Left one bloke stark bollock naked
in Elswick cemetery one night, just for the hell of it. Fancied his
suit, so he said.

Pause.

Jill Didn't you get reported?

Jean Reported? Who by? No danger of the punters reporting
us. Married, most of them. Didn't want 'the little woman'
finding out, did they? Besides, put the fear of God up them,
Micky would. Make them grateful just to be left all in one piece.

Jill So what happened?

Jean Bizzies got us. Vice squad. On the look-out for queers in
the cemetery. Got us instead.

Pause.

Spent weeks on remand. First time I'd ever been locked up,
apart from in the cupboard by me mam. Then the court.
Borstal, no messing. It was all right for Micky, he was used to it.
But me . . .

Jill You'd never been to court before?

Jean Hardly been out of the house, till I met Micky.

Pause.

Judge said I was a menace to the male population of Newcastle.

Pause.

And I was pregnant as well. Icing on the cake, that was.

Jill Pregnant?

Jean With Sharon. Had her in the Borstal, in the mother and baby unit they called it. Got married when we got out. Eighteen we were, both of us.

Jill So, did you live here?

Jean Here? Na. Only been here since the divorce. Lived all ower. Lived with his mother, lived with his so-called mates . . . Hand to mouth, most of the time. Sometimes I'd never see Micky from one week to the next. No money coming in. So I went back to Elswick Road. Only on my own. No Micky. It was what I was good at, even Micky said that. Took most of it off us, when he found out what I was doing. Left me enough for myself and Sharon, and that was it.

Jill Didn't he mind, about you . . .

Jean Na. Money for nowt, that's what he saw it as. Too busy anyway, running after other lasses. Most I ever saw of Micky was in the first year, before we got sent down. After that, it was hello, goodbye, and not much in between.

Pause.

Jill And Michael?

Jean He's Micky's.

Pause.

His boy. Can't put a foot wrong. Not like Sharon, he never had much time for her. But Michael . . .

Jill He sees Michael regularly?

Jean Oh aye, dead regular. He's got a right to, I wouldn't deny him that. But he don't really care about the bairn. He's just using the bairn to spite us.

Jill How do you mean?

Jean He's always buying him things, things he knows me and Sean can't afford. The next week, when whatever it is gets broke, he buys him something else. Always takes the bairn's side if there's an argument. Oh he checks him all right, he makes him mind when he's with *him*, but . . . outside of that, the bairn's never wrong. His boy. Do you get my meaning?

Jill Yes, I think so . . .

Jean I want what's best for Michael. Sometimes I could strangle him with my bare hands, but then I think, well it's not his fault. Not his fault he's only seven year old and such a little shit already.

Long pause.

I used to hate people like you, social workers and the like. Never used to tell them nowt, just used to clam up. Never used to let them in the house, most of them. Used to think they were ignorant, dead fuckin ignorant. Like they'd stepped out of a Christmas cake, got their eyes and ears full of currants.

Pause.

That's what I thought about you, soon as I set eyes on you. Had a friend at college who played the guitar, did you? Big fuckin deal.

Pause.

I was going to give you a hard time missy, did you know that? But then I thought, it's not her fault she's dead fuckin ignorant. Not her fault she's just stepped out of a Christmas cake. And if I clam up, she's never going to be any the wiser, is she?

Pause.

I just want what's best for Michael, that's all.

Jill And Mr Robson. Does he want what's best for Michael?

Jean Mr Robson? Mr Robson was supposed to have Michael back here for seven o'clock. Do you want another drink?

Jill No, I think . . . I think I'm all right, thank you.

Jean (*getting up*) Suit yourself. I'm having one, anyway.

Jean *exits to kitchen, returns with an opened bottle of brown ale. Sits down, pours a glass full out for herself, looks at* **Jill**. **Jill** *makes a gesture to indicate she only wants a small measure.* **Jean** *pours one out for her.*

Jean Mr Robson. It would be as well for *Mr Robson* not to know what I've just been telling you. It would be as well for you, as far as Mr Robson knows, to be still dead fuckin ignorant. Do you get my meaning?

Jill Yes, I think so. Thank you.

Jean Cos if there's one thing Mr Robson can't abide, it's people knowing too much about him. Especially the likes of you. No offence like.

Jill It's quite all right.

Jean And if he ever does find out I've been talking to you, the best place for us would be as far away from here as possible.

Jill Like Australia.

Jean I was thinking more of Gateshead, providing we'd set the Tyne on fire first. But Australia'd do for starters I suppose.

Sound of a large car pulling up outside.

Come by car did you?

Jill Yes, it's parked up at the top, on the main road. I wasn't exactly sure where your house was.

Sound of car door slamming.

Jean Should be all right up there.

Jill Yes, I left it under a lamp post.

Sound of knocking at front door. **Jean** *looks at* **Jill**, *then gets up, exits. Sound of descending. Sound of front door opening and closing. Sound of* **Jean** *and* **Micky** *ascending.* **Jean** *enters, followed by* **Micky** *carrying a child wrapped in a blanket.* **Jean** *goes to look at the child.*

Micky (*turning away*) It's all right man, he's asleep.

Micky *exits with child to bedroom one.* **Jean** *returns to sit in the armchair.* **Micky** *re-enters.*

Jean This is Miss Maybank, Michael's teacher.

Micky (*looking at himself in the mirror*) Oh aye.

Jean How come you're so late? I said to have him back by seven.

Micky (*coming to sit at left end of settee*) Michael's teacher eh?

Jill (*offering her hand, then withdrawing it when he doesn't respond*) Jill Maybank. Pleased to meet you, Mr Robson.

Micky *nods*.

Jean How come you're so late?

Micky Jeannie. Shitting and pissing herself again. Had to hang back while she got herself sorted.

Jean You should get someone in, to look after her. She's getting worse.

Micky She's all right, she can see to herself.

Jean (*to* **Jill**) It's his mother. (*To* **Micky**.) Who've you left her with?

Micky (*irritated*) Susie's stopping with her. She's all right man.

Jean Where's Maurice?

Micky Outside. Watching the car.

Jean Outside? Christ man, it's the end of November. Couldn't you have left him in it for once?

Micky Oh aye, the last time I did that he nearly had it in the Tyne.

Jean I'll get him in.

She does not move. Looks at **Micky**.

Micky Suit yourself.

Jean *gets up, exits. Sound of descending.* **Micky** *stares at* **Jill**. *She smiles, he does not respond, continues staring. Sound of front door opening.*

Jean (*off*) Ho'way man.

Sound of front door closing. Sound of **Jean** *and* **Maurice** *ascending.*

Micky Teacher eh? What'd you teach like?

Jill Everything. I take the seven year olds. I'm their class teacher.

Jean *and* **Maurice** *enter.* **Maurice** *wears a long overcoat with a Newcastle United football shirt underneath. Track suit bottoms. Badges on the overcoat. On his feet, a brand new pair of gleaming white basketball boots. Sticking out of his pockets, a roll of 'institutional' toilet paper, and several pencils. He moves with a permanent crouch, like an expectant goalkeeper.* **Jill** *glances at him in surprise, then recovers herself. During* *the remainder of the act she tries to avoid looking at him, but cannot help doing so from time to time.* **Micky** *and* **Jean** *pay no attention to him unless indicated.*

Immediately on entering **Maurice** *is transfixed by the sight of the bike. He stands gazing at it in a state of wonder, paying no attention to anything else in the room.* **Jean** *resumes her seat in the armchair.*

Micky Must see a lot of our Michael then eh?

Jill Well . . . not as much as I'd like to Mr Robson. He's not always there, you see. In school.

Micky How's that like?

Jean Ho'way man Micky, you know how that's like, it's cos he keeps wagging off man.

Micky (*ignoring* **Jean**) Been talking to her, have you, about . . . the bairn?

Maurice *reaches out cautiously, sounds the horn of the bike.*

Micky (*glancing round*) Leave it.

Maurice *turns away from the bike. Notices* **Jill** *and stands staring at her.*

Jill I've been speaking to Mrs Robson yes, that's why I called in. But I'd like to talk to you as well, to both of you in fact.

Micky Talk away.

Sound of child crying 'mam' from bedroom one. **Jean** *half rises to go to him.*

Micky Leave him.

Jean *sits down, glances briefly at* **Jill**.

Micky Like that is it?

Jean Like what man.

Micky Got it all worked out between you, have you?

He imitates her glance at **Jill**.

The little looks.

Jean *looks away in disgust.*

Watch it.

Pause.

Drive a little French car don't you, navy blue?

Jill Yes, a Renault. Why, is there . . .

Micky Nowt. Saw it parked at the top, that's all. Not a car you see a lot of around here.

Jill *smiles nervously. Sound of child crying 'mam' again.*

Micky Michael.

Maurice *starts to move slowly around the upstage half of the room, his eyes fixed on* **Jill**. *He stops whenever* **Jean** *or* **Micky** *speak, moving only when* **Jill** *speaks.*

Jill We're concerned about him, Mr Robson. The headmaster and I. Very concerned. His truanting is getting worse and when he *is* in school he's very disruptive. We've got to think of the other children. And what's best for Michael, of course.

Micky Going to have him put away are you?

Jill I'm sorry?

Micky (*mimics*) 'I want to do what's best for you, but I've got to think of the other children.' (*Normal voice.*) And the protection of the public. It's what Judges say. Just before they send you down.

Jill I don't *know* what's best for him Mr Robson, that's what we want to find out. The only thing we're sure of at the moment is that we can't go on like this. And that's why we've decided to temporarily suspend him, whilst we look at a few options.

Pause.

And in the meantime we'll arrange for him to have a home tutor, so he doesn't fall behind with his lessons. In certain situations, we often find that children who have a home tutor actually learn more than . . .

She trails off, looking at **Micky**, *who has been staring at her. Pause.*

Jean Well say something man, for Christ's sake. What'd you think?

Micky (*still looking at* **Jill**) Why bother to ask me? Sounds like you've got it all nicely worked out between you.

Jean It's nowt to do with me. It wasn't worked out with me.

Micky (*looking at* **Jean**) I didn't mean *you*. Christ, you have enough trouble working out whether it's a cock you're sucking on or your own tit. I meant her and her mates at the school, looking at their *options*.

Jean So that's it, is it?

Micky Like I say, looks like *they've* got it all worked out between them. Like *they* always have. In certain situations.

Sound of a child crying 'mam' again.

Jill It's not like that at all Mr Robson, it's . . .

Micky (*interrupting*) See to him for Christ's sake.

Jean *gets up, exits to bedroom one.* **Micky** *puts his feet up on the coffee table.*

Micky Been up here long have you, in Newcastle?

Jill About three months. I came up at the start of the autumn term. Look, about Michael, he's . . .

Micky (*to* **Maurice**) Come and sit down man, do your words.

Maurice *comes to kneel at the left end of the coffee table. Takes out a pencil and the roll of toilet paper, which he carefully unrolls. There are a number of words already written on it in pencil. He continues unrolling it until he has found a clear space.*

Jill Look, about Michael, he's . . .

Micky (*interrupting*) Boyfriend moved up yet has he?

Jill I'm sorry?

Micky Boyfriend. Tall bloke with glasses. Carries his stuff about in one of them big red bags with straps. Moved up yet has he?

Maurice *finds his place, then begins to write down occasional words from their conversation, pronouncing them aloud to himself as he does so. When he is not doing this, he mouths words to himself silently.*

Maurice (*writing*) Boyfriend. B – oy – friend. Boyfriend.

Jill I'm sorry, I don't know what you mean.

Micky Oh I see. So you didn't meet this bloke at the station a couple of weeks ago and drive him back to your little place in Gosforth?

Maurice (*writing, concentrating hard*) Bloke. Bl – o – ke. Bloke.

Micky *pats* **Maurice** *on the head.*

Jill Look, I . . .

Micky It was Michael told me it was you. We were driving around town one Friday after school. He spotted you. In your little blue car. 'That's my teacher!' So we followed you, just for a laugh. Dead excited about it, Michael was. Good at it too, kept well out of sight. Got a lot of weeds in your front garden mind. Probably too busy for gardening, eh? Regent Terrace, isn't it?

Maurice (*writing*) Busy. Bi – zee. Busy.

Jill Look . . .

Micky Well, I'm looking. Quite nice. Reckon you could do better for yourself than that bloke with the glasses, don't you? Drink at the Gosforth do you? How about tomorrow night, half past seven? See you in there, huh?

Maurice (*writing*) Bloke. Bl – o – ke. Bloke.

Jill Look Mr Robson . . .

Micky Micky. Call me Micky, Jill.

Takes his feet off the table, holds out his hand towards her. She does not take it.

Oh I see. Bit too rough for you, is that it?

He looks down at his hands.

Tattoos not suit? Pity. I had a special message put on them, just for you.

Holds out his left hand, the knuckles towards her. She is repelled, but looks at it.

Jill (*reading his knuckles*) L, T, F, C . . . I don't understand. Is it a football team?

Micky *does the same with his right hand.*

Jill (*reading*) E, S, U, K . . . I still don't understand.

He puts his knuckles together, holds them towards her.

Jill (*reading*) Lets . . .

Micky Fuck. That's the other word. Lets fuck. Understand what it says now, do you?

He takes his hands away.

Maurice Fuck.

Micky Saves a lot of time. In certain situations.

Pause / **Jill** *looks at the door of bedroom one.*

Maurice Fuck. F – u – ck. Fuck.

Micky Don't say a lot do you? In certain situations.

Pause.

Jill Look, the only thing I've come to talk to you about is Michael. Anything else . . . well, I'm sorry, but I'm not interested. I'm sorry to be rude, but . . .

Micky (*interrupting*) Oh, sorry to be rude is it? Do it with the lights out do you, with yer woolly tights on? Or is that still too rude for you?

She looks away. **Micky** *gets up, walks downstage, turns to face her.*

Micky Rude. What do you know about being rude? Probably drop down dead if you stood on someone's foot in the bus queue. Oh *sorry*, I was forgetting, you don't stand in bus queues do you? Got a little blue car haven't you? Parked up at the top, isn't it?

Maurice (*writing*) Dead. D – ea – d. Dead.

Micky I'll tell you what I think about your sort, in *all* fucking situations. It's not that you're too rude. What sticks in my fucking craw is *you're never rude enough*. YOU'RE ALWAYS FUCKING APOLOGISING.

Picks up video control.

And it means nothing to you. Options. You might as well be pressing buttons on this fucking machine.

Flicks the control.

I'm sorry, don't want your sort in here, too *disruptive*. Have to *suspend* you, I reckon. Never mind, let's try the *options*.

Flicks control.

Oh dear. It's come up with . . . putting him away. Only we call it *care*. Sorry about that.

Flicks control.

Oh dear, what's this? This wife's gone off it cos her man's away. Can't manage. Dumped one of her kids in the Assistance. Left him (*Indicates* **Maurice**.) sitting on the counter, poor little cunt. No, don't call him that, it's not right. I mean, cunt's useful. He isn't. Never mind, try the *options*.

Flicks control.

Oh dear, it's come up with . . . putting him away. Sorry about that. Better take his brother as well, just to be on the safe side. It's all for the best, they'll soon get used to it.

Flicks control.

Now what. Brother (*Indicates* **Maurice**.) got a slate blown off. Never mind, let's have a look.

Flicks control.

Funny, can't seem to find it anywhere. Never mind, he'll be all right. Just don't let him out in the rain, that's all. Better still, just don't let him out. Don't worry, you'll manage. Let us know if you need any help.

He pauses, looking at her.

Maurice (*writing*) Help. H – el – p. Help.

Micky Ever ask yourself why the ignorant fuckers put up with it? Ever wonder that do you, when you're sitting on your arse in your office, having a quick wank through your options?

He throws the control down on the table.

Jill I'm sorry, I don't have an office, I . . .

Micky DON'T KEEP SAYING SORRY!

Jean *comes out of bedroom one, stands watching.* **Micky** *glances at her, then sits down as before.*

Micky Come on down. Join the fucking party why don't you.

Jean (*returning to armchair*) Knocked you back did she?

Maurice (*writing*) S – o – rry. Sorry.

Micky *looks at what* **Maurice** *is writing.*

Micky Hey man your spelling is getting worse. (*To* **Jill**.) Want to come and have a look over his spelling?

Jill No. No thank you.

Micky (*to* **Jean**) Eee, she's knocked us back again. (*Abrupt change, much harder.*) Watch your mouth.

Maurice (*writing*) Mouth. M – ou – th. Mouth.

Jill (*to* **Micky**) Do *you* wonder why they put up with it?

Micky No, I don't. Put up with anything when you're fucking dead, don't you?

Jill I'm . . . I don't understand. What do you mean?

Jean (*to* **Jill**) Don't listen to him man, he's only trying to needle you cos you wouldn't let him get his leg over.

Micky Oh, so it's *man* now is it? Big mates? (*Scornful.*) Leg over.

Pause.

You've changed your tune haven't you? Time was when you wouldn't let a fucking social worker in the house.

Jean Well she's not a fucking social worker is she?

Micky What's got into you? (*Suddenly roars.*) THEY'RE ALL THE FUCKING SAME MAN.

Maurice *crouches down, hands over his ears.*

Jean OH NO THEY'RE NOT. YOU NOTICED IT YOURSELF. (*Pointing at* **Jill** *in mock amazement.*) LOOK, THIS ONE'S GOT TITS!

Micky *stares at her, then begins chuckling to himself. Notices* **Maurice** *and pats the top of his head.*

Micky It's all right man, she's just away with the fucking mixer.

Maurice *uncovers his ears, but remains crouching and subdued.* **Micky** *gets up, still feigning amusement.*

Jean (*to* **Jill**) Sorry.

Jill *makes a gesture to indicate 'it's all right'.*

Micky (*sauntering upstage, not looking at them*) That's her word man. Christ, you're even starting to talk like them.

Looks at himself in the mirror.

Jean Checking to make sure you're still here?

Micky Oh, I'm still here all right.

Jill (*looking at her watch*)   I think perhaps I ought to go.

Micky (*quietly*)   Stay where you are.

Jill *looks at* **Jean**, *who shakes her head*.

Micky   You asked me a question.

Pause.

You asked me what I meant.

Jill   About them putting up with it . . .

Micky   Because they're dead.

Maurice (*not writing, still frightened*)   Duh . . . duh.

Micky (*coming back downstage*)   Ever walked round here in daylight? Ever got out of your little car and walked around here?

Jill   I'm a teacher, we don't . . .

Micky (*interrupting*)   Thought not.

*Pause / **Micky** looks out over the audience.*

Jill   I'm a *teacher*, we don't . . .

Micky (*interrupting*)   So you've never noticed all the houses boarded up. How everything's grey, or brown. No curtains at the windows. Just faces, watching you. And nobody walking about. Just a few kids and dogs, and that's it. Or maybe there's a gang of lads trying to tidy up the place with a bloke watching them, kids doing a piddly-shit job for piddly-shit money. Never noticed how they always leave someone in the house, 'cos they're shit scared some fucker's going to break in and pinch whatever it is they haven't got. How they never open the door if they don't know who you are. Just want to sit like slugs waiting for their giros to come. Like they're not alive. Dead.

Pause.

Jill (*quietly*)   I didn't kill them, Mr Robson.

Micky   And then you come on the scene. Or someone like you. From Gosforth. From Jesmond. From some other fucking planet. Like vultures flying over the desert. And you see all this . . . shit. Now what? Don't want to get your hands messed up. I mean, you've got to go back to that nice little house in Gosforth, haven't you? So you put on your rubber gloves and you just . . . (*Gesture.*) . . . rearrange it. You move this pile of shit to over there. Tidy it up a bit. Sort out the dead from the nearly dead.

Just like vultures. Take this kid into care cos he's not going to school, get this wife another three quid on her giro. And they just stand there, gobstruck. Like . . . uhhhh. While you just faff about, like a fart in a thunderstorm. Writing everything down. Wanting to know the ins and outs of a duck's arse hole. And they tell you . . . uhhhh.

He turns to face them.

And then you fly back up to the sky. Leaving all the shit behind you. Only now it's in smaller piles.

Jill And what do I . . . we . . . get out of all this?

Micky Cash. Nice and clean, straight into the bank account. Enough to buy that little house and that little car and a holiday away once in a while. Somewhere nice and quiet, just like you. But not *too* much money, cos that might make people think you don't really *care*.

Jill And I don't really care at all, is that what you're trying to say?

Micky Oh you care all right. You care so fucking much. Which is the other thing you get out of it, more than the cash I reckon. That feeling inside when you're sitting at home of a night, sipping your dry white wine (not too expensive). Watching the tele, all them pictures of starving kids. How you're really somebody. Cos you *care*, and you're doing something about it. Not like them moneygrabbing fuckers down South, roaring around in their BM fucking W's. *They* don't give a fuck, anyone can see that. But you do. Oh, you care all right. Why, you even buy your clothes at the fucking Oxfam shop, don't you?

Jill You should go into politics.

Micky Oh I'm in politics. I'm in politics all right. Only it's a party of one. So I don't have to wait for some prat coming on the tele and saying what he'll do if I put my cross on his bit of paper. Cos it always gets bent. Like saying *suspend* instead of coming straight out with it, that you want to put him away. Cos that's what you'll do. After six months of farting on about *options*. That's what you'll do all right.

Pause.

Politics. It's you who's in politics. And she . . . (*Pointing at* **Jean**.) . . . SHE FUCKING BELIEVES YOU.

Maurice *covers his ears, crouching as low as possible.*

Micky (*walking upstage*) There's only one sort of people I trust, and that's the fucking polis. Cos with them at least you know where you fuckin stand. Which is nowhere, no fucking where at all. They don't just *bend* the truth, like your lot. No, *they* make things up out of thin air, just to get you downstairs. But at least you know where you fucking stand.

Maurice *cautiously uncovers his head, returns to kneeling position.*

Micky (*laughing, to* **Jean**) I didn't tell you this. Solicitor told us yesterday, we was going through the committal papers. They had down . . . (*Imitating a policeman.*) . . . 'When arrested, Robson had on an SAS type mask and was wearing socks over his hands' . . . (*Scornfully.*) . . . socks over his hands . . . we're supposed to be the best team in the fucking North . . . don't you think we could have afforded gloves?

Shakes his head, laughing. **Maurice** *suddenly laughs, stops abruptly.*

Jill You're wrong. About Michael.

Pause / **Micky** *looks at her.*

I don't want to see him taken into care. And you're wrong about the vultures as well. If that was true I wouldn't be here now. It's because I *don't* want to see him taken into care that I'm sitting here talking to you at nearly eight o'clock on a Friday night.

Pause / **Micky** *makes a dismissive gesture.*

But that wouldn't be anything to do with me in any case. You see, it's . . .

Micky (*interrupting*) Never is anything to do with you is it, it's always some other fucker *back at the office*. Like when me mother dumped him (*Indicates* **Maurice**.) in the Assistance. Four year old he were. I was seven, just like Michael is now. Never done nowt, same as Michael. So they put *him* (*Indicates* **Maurice**.) in a home, 'cos he's backward, and his mother can't cope, and then . . .

Maurice *covers his ears.*

And then some *prick* with a fucking briefcase . . . no, couldn't have been a prick 'cos it was a bloke . . . they don't have pricks do they, that sort of bloke . . . must have been a prat . . . so this *prat* with a fucking briefcase comes and says 'I'm sorry Mrs Robson but little John Michael' . . . I'm Micky to the rest of the world but he calls me John Michael . . . 'I'm sorry but little John

Michael will have to go away as well, for *assessment* . . . just for a week or two, while we sort out what's best for you and the family'.

He advances on **Jill**. **Maurice** *crouches right down, his hands still over his ears.*

And how long was I away for, just because she dumped *him* in the Assistance? How long did it take them to do their fucking assessment? ELEVEN FUCKING YEARS.

Turns away, then comes back, still angry.

So don't fucking come it, right? We don't want your help. We need cash, we'll get it ourselves. We fall sick, we'll get ourselves well. Don't call us, we'll call you. Only we won't.

Pause.

All right, Miss Oxford and Cambridge?

Jill Sheffield actually.

Micky What?

Jill Sheffield. I don't come from Oxford or Cambridge. I come from Sheffield.

Micky I knew it was one of them places down South.

Jean It's not down South man. It's up here somewhere. Just past Middlesbrough.

Micky Oh it's just past *Middlesbrough* is it? Well I thought *you'd* know. Probably been down there have you, with that daft Denise? (*To* Jill.) Been quite a one, has Mrs Robson. Likes the batter, you see. Had more pricks than the dartboard at the West End Social. Got quite a name for it she has. Only I wouldn't use it here, seeing we're in such polite company. (*Scornfully.*) Sheffield.

Jill It's not that far away.

Micky It's far enough. Ever noticed that, have you? That it's never *round here* that you lot come from? Always from somewhere else. Like vultures flying over. And nesting. In Gosforth. In Jesmond. All them nice places. Full of nice people like you. Never here. Here's where you suck the blood. That right, Miss Sheffield? Where's *your* home in the West?

Maurice *cautiously takes his hands from his ears and returns to a kneeling position.*

Jill I don't *have* to come from round here. I don't *have* to live here. I can still . . .

Micky (*interrupting*) Can you?

Pause.

Jean Where's yours?

Micky Where's my what?

Jean Where's *your* home in the West? You don't live here.

Micky Oh that's right. I was forgetting. I live in Blakelaw. A million fucking miles away Blakelaw is. Or is it three?

Jean It's still not here though.

Micky (*behind the settee, leaning over* **Jill**, *looking at* **Jean**) And the reason it's not here, suckface, is cos I got out. Escaped. The only way you can from here. (*Transferring to* **Jill**.) Well, one of three ways. You make a fuckin pop record, so thousands of daft buggers like Sharon'll come screaming after you, or, you kick a ball about a daft bit of grass, or, you do what I do. And if you don't make it, if your record don't sell or you break your fuckin leg, it'll always be ready for you, your home in the West. All nicely boarded up. And there's always vacancies. Cos sure as fuck no other fucker wants to live here. (*His face against hers.*) Like my aftershave?

Jill I wondered what that smell was.

Long pause / they stare at each other.

So, if you don't sing or play football, what do you do?

Maurice *looks up suddenly.*

Micky (*walking upstage*) That's my business.

Maurice (*looking at* **Jill**, *strong emphasis on words, not writing them down*) Foot – ball. Foot – ball.

Jean That's started him off now, football.

Jill So what is your business, Mr Robson?

Micky It's whatever she's told you it is. It's . . .

Maurice (*interrupting, still looking at* **Jill**) Foot – ball.

Micky It's not being fucking dead, that's what it is. (*Looking in mirror, rubbing his face.*) Like my aftershave?

Jean You're wasting your time man, she's not interested.

Micky (*puts his hands together, looks at his knuckles*) There's not a pair of knickers in Newcastle can hold out against me.

Jean Well there is one pair.

Micky Taken to wearing knickers now have you? (*Turns away, stands facing upstage.*) I wouldn't crawl across her to get to you, and that's for fucking sure.

Maurice Foot – ball.

Jean (*to* **Jill**) It always sets him off, football.

Jill Sorry, I didn't . . .

Maurice (*interrupting*) Supermac. Supermac.

Jean Na man, ho'way.

Maurice (*screwing up his face in concentration, still looking at* **Jill**) Kee – gan. Kee – gan.

Jean Na man, that's years ago. Ho'way.

Pause.

Maurice (*as before, with slow grin of triumph*) Mi – ra.

Pause. He says the words slowly at first, then gradually speeds up.

Mi – ra. Mi – ra.

Pause.

Mira Mira Mira Mira Mira Mira!

Pauses, then proudly opens his jacket to show **Jill** *his shirt.*

Mira Mira Mira Mira Mira . . . Gazza!

Pause.

Mira Gazza Mira Gazza Mira Gazza!

Remains in pose, holding open his jacket.

Jean (*to* **Jill**) Footballers. Newcastle.

Jill Oh.

Micky (*turning round, beckoning* **Maurice**) Come here.

Maurice *stands up, runs over to* **Micky**.

Jean Micky, don't hurt him man.

Micky (*taking hold of* **Maurice** *by the collar, turning him round to face* **Jill**) I'm not going to hurt him. I just thought that teacher here might like to see our Maurice do his party piece. (*To* **Maurice**.) Ho'way man, do your song.

Maurice *stands with furrowed brow, concentrating.* **Micky** *continues to hold him by the collar.*

Micky Ho'way man.

Maurice *turns to* **Micky**, *makes gesture to indicate he needs help to start.*

Maurice Um. Um.

Jean You need to start him off man.

Micky (*ignoring her*) Ready?

Maurice Um.

Micky (*singing, loud but tuneful*) We've got . . .

He jerks **Maurice***'s head.*

Maurice MRNDAA!

Micky (*to* **Jill**, *speaking*) We've got Mirandinha. (*To* **Maurice**, *singing.*) He's not from . . .

He jerks **Maurice***'s head.*

Maurice ARGNTAA!

Micky (*to* **Jill**, *speaking*) He's not from Argentina. (*To* **Maurice**, *singing.*) He's from . . .

Jerks.

Maurice BRZLL!

Micky (*to* **Jill**, *speaking*) He's from Brazil. (*To* **Maurice**, *singing.*) And he's fucking fucking . . .

Maurice (*excited, roaring*) BRILL!

They sing the song again, straight through this time, **Maurice** *joining in as before. As the last line is reached,* **Micky** *suddenly runs* **Maurice** *towards* **Jill**. *They end up immediately behind her,* **Micky** *shoving* **Maurice***'s head in her direction.*

Micky Want a souvenir of your visit? Take one of the natives home with you? Think he'd go down well in Gosforth?

*He pushes **Maurice***'s head into her face.

Look, never been used, nothing on the clock apart from the maker's name.

*He pushes **Maurice** away. **Maurice** goes to the table, kneels down and picks up his paper and pencil.*

Micky Only they had to sharp charge that cos they weren't getting many orders. Not once people had seen that one. Can't think why. Fancy a souvenir?

Maurice (*looking at his words and shouting them out to* **Jill**, *his speech more slurred than previously*) BOY – FRIEND. BLOKE.

Jean Christ man you're really set him off now.

Maurice BU – SY. BLOKE.

Micky (*going to left wall*) Bit too much for you? How about something else? Nice piece of wallpaper?

Starts to rip pieces of wallpaper off the wall.

Maurice FUCK ... DEAD ... HELP.

Jean (*turning away*) Fuckin seen it all now.

Maurice (*stands up, gesturing to* **Jill**) HELP ... SO – RRY.

Micky (*holding wallpaper*) Go nicely? In Gosforth?

Maurice (*going to stand in front of* **Jill**) SO – RRY ... MOUTH.

Micky (*looking at wallpaper*) Reckon not somehow. Oh well. Pity about that.

Maurice SO – RRY ... MOUTH.

Jean Quite finished have you?

Micky Reckon so. Ho'way man.

Maurice (*backing away from* **Jill** *towards* **Micky**, *but still looking at her*) So – rry. Mouth.

He continues to mouth the words silently.

Micky (*to* **Jill**, *taking* **Maurice** *by the collar again*) And about Michael. He'll be at school Monday morning no problem. No more running away. Won't want to lose the bike you see. Soon cure him, that bike will.

Jill But he's suspended, that's what I've come to . . .

Micky Come? Save that for the boyfriend if I were you. Wouldn't come here again. No point, if Michael's going to school. Don't suppose I'll be seeing you again, unless you're in the Gosforth tomorrow night of course. Won't shake hands. Been doing a spot of wallpapering. (*To* **Maurice**.) Ho'way.

He wheels **Maurice** *round towards the door, then lets go of him.* **Maurice** *stands transfixed by the sight of the bike.* **Micky** *starts to the door without him, then pauses and turns.*

Micky Want a lift? Up to the top?

Jill No thank you . . . I want to have a few words with Mrs Robson.

Micky Oh I see. Funny, I thought you were ready to go there before. Must have picked you up wrong. Looks like you're stuck here for a while then.

Jill How do you mean?

Micky Well, never know who you might run into on your own do you? Criminals, rapists, football hooligans, could meet any of them around here. Not like Gosforth. Still, give you a chance to get to know the area, sitting here with Jean. Quiet now, but it'll warm up later on. Bit of an education for you. Be able to tell that bloke with the glasses all about it. (*To* **Maurice**.) Ho'way man.

Maurice *turns and suddenly runs past* **Micky**, *exits down the stairs.* **Micky** *follows, going straight out without looking back. Sound of them descending, then front door opening and being slammed shut. Car door opens and slams, twice. Car starts up, drives away.*

Jean He's a little treasure. Should be dug and buried.

Pause.

Fancy another drink?

Jill I'd better not as I'm driving.

Jean (*getting up, going into the kitchen*) Not yet you're not.

Jill Did he mean that, about not going out?

Jean (*returning with opened bottle of brown ale*) He means everything. He has to make people afraid of him. That's why he said that. He wants to have you sitting here all night on your fanny, wondering if he's out there waiting for you somewhere.

Meanwhiles he'll be out on the town more than likely, clubbing it. Best not chance it though. I'll walk you up to the top when Sharon gets back.

Pours the brown ale into the two glasses, gives **Jill** *one and sips the other herself.*

Like he said, it's a lesson for you. Make you think before you come down here the next time. On your own in the dark.

Jill I should have realised. Stupid of me.

Jean *shrugs.*

Jill Is he like that . . . to all women?

Jean You made it worse for yourself. By knocking him back like that.

Pause.

Not that there's owt else you could have done like. I mean, he's not exactly your type I suppose.

Jill Perhaps not.

Jean Probably fancied a change from the usual. Never been out with one of your sort more than likely. Probably wanted to see if you had everything in the same place as the rest of us.

Jill It must have been hard living with him.

Jean Feels like I still am sometimes. Cos he never lets go of you.

Jill How do you mean?

Jean If you're a woman, you're either a slag or his mother. It's either fuck or suck. I used to be the one, now I'm mostly the other. Me and Jeannie, that's his proper mother, we share it between us. Fuck or suck.

Sound of breaking glass outside.

Don't worry about your car. It'll be all right more than likely. If it's under a lamp.

Lights fade to black.

Intermission.

Act Three

Lights fade up to reveal the set as at the end of Act Two. The clock now shows eleven. Empty glasses and brown ale bottles on the coffee table. Sound of two people coming upstairs. **Sharon** *and* **Jean** *enter,* **Jean** *shivering with cold.* **Sharon** *sits at the left end of the settee.* **Jean** *comes down centre to warm herself by the fire.*

Jean Christ it's cold out there. Glad you got back early mind. How's Mandy?

Sharon Aw reet. Will she be all right, Miss Maybank?

Jean (*going to sit on arm of the armchair*) Aye, I told her to keep to the main roads.

Sharon What happened to the wallpaper?

Jean Just your dad working himself again. Thought he'd do a bit of decorating, I think that's what he called it.

Pause.

Sharon What's going to happen about Michael?

Jean How the fuckin hell should I know Sharon?

Pause.

I don't know. Teacher reckons he's suspended. Micky reckons he's going to school. Come Monday morning, neither of them'll be fuckin here and Jean Robson'll have to work it out for herself. As usual.

Sharon So what's . . .

Jean I DON'T FUCKING KNOW SHARON, ALL RIGHT?

Pause.

ALL RIGHT?

Sharon All right.

Pause.

I was just . . .

Jean Well don't.

Pause.

I'm just waiting on Sean coming back and then I'm going to bed. I've had enough talking for one day, all right?

Sharon All right.

Pause.

Can't we have the tele on?

Jean It's on the blink.

Sharon What about the video?

Jean IT'S ON THE FUCKING BLINK. CHRIST MAN, WHAT'S GOT INTO YOU?

Sharon Nowt's got into me.

Pause.

What's got into you more like.

Jean Don't be so fuckin cheeky.

Pause.

Sharon Mandy's mam was at the club.

Pause.

She said Sean was on, doing his song and that.

Pause.

She said it were all right, like.

Jean So it should be, he's been fuckin practising it enough.

Sharon She said it went down well like.

Jean Don't say that, he'll never get his head through the fuckin door. Still, Micky got his through, so I suppose Sean'll manage.

Pause.

Sharon How come you're always picking on him?

Jean Who, Sean?

Sharon Uh huh.

Jean Picking on *Sean? Me?* Picking on *him?* (*Gets up, walks up centre.*) That's good, that is. (*Turns to face downstage.*) And what gave you that fucking idea?

Sharon What.

Jean That I'm always picking on Sean.

Sharon Nowt. Just that you're always slagging him off.

Jean You want to keep your nose out.

Pause.

All right?

Sharon All right.

Jean (*to herself*) Picking on him. (*To* **Sharon**.) You want to keep your nose out.

Heavy knocking at front door.

Jean Answer the door.

Sharon You're the nearest.

Jean Don't be so cheeky. Answer the fuckin door.

Sharon *gets up quickly and exits in a huff.* **Jean** *remains standing up centre. Sound of descending, sound of door opening.*

Sharon (*off*) It's Sean.

Pause.

Get off man.

Jean (*turning towards the door*) SEAN!

Sound of door closing.

Sharon (*off, louder*) Get *off* man.

Sound of **Sharon** *ascending quickly, followed more slowly by* **Sean**. **Sharon** *enters without looking at* **Jean**, *quickly resumes her seat on the settee.* **Sean** *reaches the top of the stairs. Sound of him falling over the boots.*

Jean Now what.

Sean (*off*) Jesus. Me own boots come back to haunt us.

Enter **Sean**, *swaying slightly, carrying his guitar case.*

Sean And God said, let there be boots, and there were boots. Hello my love.

Pause / **Jean** *does not respond.*

And God looked upon the boots and saw that they were good. Christ we've got a fine field of potatoes here said God. (*Comes down left.*) Play your boots right and you could be playing for Newcastle in next to no time. United we stand. You'll never walk alone. (*Notices the ripped wallpaper.*) Christ. Was anybody hurt in this accident?

*Pause / **Sean** looks round.*

I said, was anybody hurt . . .

Jean We heard.

Sean (*looking at wall*) Christ, I'm too good for this place. (*Puts down guitar case, turns to face them.*) So.

Jean So what.

Sean So ask me how it was.

Pause.

Sharon So how was it.

Jean You keep your nose out. (*Resigned.*) So how was it?

Sean Christ, did I hear someone ask me how it was? It was . . .

Pauses, searching for words.

Jean You managed to get pissed then.

Sean Jean, your powers of observation never cease to amaze. (*Catches sight of himself in the mirror.*) All done . . . by mirrors. It was . . . the warmth of the people. That's what it was, the warmth of the people.

Jean Oh aye.

Sean They took me. To their hearts. Have a drink Sean. Have another drink. Not 'where's your wage packet'.

Jean What's that supposed to mean?

Sean Not take the whole wage packet and here's a fiver for yourself.

Jean Christ man, if I let you keep the money it'd all be gone on the Friday night, you know that.

Sean *makes a dismissive gesture.*

Ho'way to bed man, if all you're going to do is cause arguments.

Sean Aye, it's a wonder you haven't started charging for that, going to bed with you.

Jean Jesus.

Sean I mean, you're well known for it, charging. It's a wonder you haven't started charging me.

Jean Not in front of the bairn man.

Sean Bairn? I see no bairn. Is not the bairn asleep, even now dreaming of dead cats with fifty pence pieces in their eye sockets? I see no bairn.

Jean I meant Sharon man.

Sean Oh, Sharon is it? Now there's a thing. I would never have guessed. That you were talking about Sharon I mean.

Walks unsteadily around the front of the settee and sits down, leaving space between himself and **Sharon**.

Well, well, well. (*To* **Sharon**.) That's the story of the three holes in the ground. (*Picks up bottles and examines them.*) All empty.

Jean (*coming up behind him*) Well she's still at school. She's still a bairn isn't she?

Sean Ah, now there's a thing. She's been taking *lessons* all right. Or maybe she hasn't. Maybe it's in the blood. Like mother, like . . . Sharon. No, bairn's not the right word.

Pause.

There is a word, only she doesn't charge for it you see, so you can't use . . . that particular word.

Pause.

No, I'd just call her 'the flower of the West End'. Only she's been plucked. Been plucked quite a few times tonight eh Sharon? About time you started bringing home a bit cash, like yer mam.

There is a sudden explosion of shouting between the three of them.

Jean (*to* **Sharon**) What the fuckin hell is he on about?

Sharon Nowt.

Sean Oh aye?

Jean (*going towards* **Sharon**) I said what . . .

Sharon *Nowt* man, he's just jealous that's all.

Sean Jealous!

Sharon He saw us talkin to some lads. When he was going to the club.

Sean Talkin!

Sharon Aye, talkin!

Jean I thought you were going to Mandy's?

Sharon I was. I was on my way to Mandy's.

Jean She only lives just over the back.

Sean You want to listen to the crack about her at the club.

Jean What crack?

Sharon He's just making it up man, cos I wouldn't let him.

Jean Wouldn't let him what?

Sean Wouldn't touch your arse with the toe of me boot.

Sharon He's always after us, carrying on and that.

Jean When's this?

Sharon When you're not here.

Sean Ho'way!

Sharon You *are*.

Jean You bastard.

Jean *goes to hit* **Sean**. *He grabs hold of her and pulls her down, so that she is half sprawled over the settee. He grabs a glass from the coffee table, breaks it and holds it against her face. Outside, there is a screech of brakes as a large car pulls up. They do not notice it.*

Sean Oh aye? Now we'll hear the fuckin truth. (*To* **Sharon**.) Tell it.

Pause / **Sean** *moves the glass closer to* **Jean**'s *face.*

Tell it.

Thunderous knocking at front door.

Jean Micky!

Sean (*to* **Sharon**) Leave it.

More thunderous knocking.

Jean MICKY!

Sean Fuckin leave it, right?

Jean MICKY!!!

There is a crash as the front door is kicked in. Sound of **Micky** *rushing upstairs.* **Sean** *jumps up, the glass still in his hand.* **Jean** *is still sprawled over the settee,* **Sharon** *recoiled at left end of it.* **Micky** *enters at a run.*

Micky Oh aye?

Sean (*pointing glass at* **Micky**) Don't.

Micky Oh aye?

Sean *makes a dive for the bathroom door but trips over the armchair. As he regains his balance he is intercepted by* **Micky**, *who knocks the glass out of his hand and disables him with two swift punches to the stomach. As* **Sean** *goes down,* **Micky** *grabs him by the scruff of the neck and propels him across the room towards the stairs, then throws him down them. Sound of* **Sean** *falling downstairs. Sound of* **Micky** *kicking the boots downstairs after him.* **Micky** *stands looking down the stairs for a moment, then turns back into the room. As he speaks, it is obvious that the fight with* **Sean** *is already dismissed from his mind.*

Micky Jeannie.

Jean (*getting to her feet*) Christ man you might have killed him.

Sharon Probably *has* killed him.

Micky Jeannie man.

Jean What about her?

Micky She's sick. Had one of her turns.

Jean What'd you want me to do?

Micky Take a look at her.

Jean What now? Where is she?

Micky Outside.

Jean Outside?

Micky Outside in the car.

Jean Christ. Well I suppose you'd better bring her in then.

Micky *looks at her, exits. Sound of descending.*

Jean (*to* **Sharon**) Get to bed.

*Sharon exits to bedroom one. Sound of Micky and Maurice
ascending. Enter Micky carrying Jeannie wrapped in a blanket.
Behind him Maurice, quietly whimpering to himself. He hovers behind
the settee, constantly shifting from one foot to the other, his hands making
small fluttering movements. Micky lays Jeannie on the settee, her head
stage right. All that is visible of her is the back of her head and her
slippers; the rest of her body is covered by the blanket. Micky sits on the
left arm of the settee. Jean sits at the other end, bends over Jeannie.*

Micky (*staring ahead*) How is she?

Jean Give us a chance. (*Looks at Jeannie's face and then takes one
of her hands.*) How long's she been like this?

Micky Bout an hour.

Pause.

Maybe a bit longer. (*Turns towards her.*) Why, what difference
does it make?

Jean Didn't you think of calling the doctor?

Micky Na.

Jean Why not?

Micky What'd you mean why not?

Jean Why didn't you call for the friggin doctor?

Micky (*turning back to stare straight ahead*) Don't have no truck
with doctors, you know that.

Pause.

Just want to put her in a home, doctors.

Pause.

Would have put her in a home straightaway.

Pause.

Jean So what were you doing all that time?

Micky Trying to bring her round. Same as last time it
happened. Trying to warm her up.

Pause.

Worked last time.

Pause.

Just taking a bit longer that's all.

Pause.

Doctors.

Pause.

Jean So why'd you bring her round here?

Pause.

Thought I could bring her round when you couldn't, is that it?

Micky (*turning*) Well you're a fucking woman aren't you?

Jean (*standing up, coming down right*) I may be a woman but I'm not fucking Jesus.

Pause.

I can't raise the dead Micky.

Long pause.

Maurice Dead . . . dead.

Micky (*turning*) SHUT IT.

Maurice (*to himself*) Dead.

His movements gradually become more agitated.

Micky (*staring straight ahead*) She's not fucking dead.

Jean She is Micky, she's cold.

Micky WELL TRY WARMING HER UP THEN.

Jean WHAT'S THE FRIGGIN POINT MICKY WHEN YOU'VE BEEN DOING THE EXACT SAME THING FOR THE PAST HOUR, AND IT HASN'T WORKED?

Pause.

Micky You're a woman. It might work for you.

Jean You're away with the friggin mixer, man.

Pause.

If you'd have sent for the doctor in the first place . . .

Micky WELL I DIDN'T, RIGHT?

Jean Right.

Pause / **Maurice** *runs, stops.*

Micky She don't like doctors.

Jean SO IT'S HER FAULT NOW IS IT?

Micky What.

Jean HER FAULT YOU DIDN'T SEND FOR A DOCTOR, COS SHE DIDN'T LIKE THEM? HO'WAY.

Pause / **Maurice** *runs, stops.*

Micky They were sniffing around last week, trying to put her in a home.

Pause.

She wanted nowt to do with them.

Jean Kept right out of it did you? Left it up to her did you?

Pause.

You were the one told them to fuck off man, she told me so herself.

Pause.

Wouldn't even let them send a nurse in regular, to check up on her.

Micky I DIDN'T WANT THEM SNIFFIN AROUND MAN.

Jean *You* didn't want them sniffin around, what about her?

Pause / **Maurice** *runs, stops.*

Micky She'll be all right.

Jean What you going to do, go across the other side and bring her back?

Pause.

It's not fuckin Gateshead she's gone to, Micky.

Micky (*trying to remain controlled*) She'll be all right.

Jean SHE'S FUCKIN DEAD MAN.

Micky WELL DO SOMETHING ABOUT IT.

Maurice *runs.*

AND STOP FUCKIN RUNNING ABOUT FOR CHRIST'S SAKE.

Maurice *stops.*

Jean (*voice breaking*) HE'S FUCKIN UPSET MAN. (*Goes and sits on arm of the armchair.*) Jesus Christ.

Pause.

Jean (*tossing her head back, regaining control*) She's dead, I can't do anything about it. She's dead.

Pause.

Micky We don't take help from no one. Fuck em.

Jean Christ Micky, there's a difference in not having social workers sniffin round the doors and not sending for a doctor when your own mother's . . .

Pause.

Jesus Christ.

Micky (*getting up, coming down left, staring downstage*) To you there is. Cos you're soft. To me, there isn't.

Jean So people have to friggin die, so you can prove you don't need help?

Pause.

Micky She'll be all right.

Pause.

She's just sleeping it off. Like the last time.

Jean *goes over to sit at right end of the settee, uncovers* **Jeannie***'s head, shakes her gently.*

Jean Jeannie?

Pause.

Jeannie?

Pause. She covers **Jeannie** *over, looks up at* **Micky***.*

Well?

Long pause.

Maurice Dead, dead.

He starts running about, towards **Jeannie** *and away again, gradually getting closer.*

Jean (*returning to armchair*) You've killed her Micky. You've killed her to prove a fuckin point.

Pause.

Well I believe you. You don't need anybody. You've fuckin proved it.

Long pause. By now **Maurice** *has come right up to* **Jeannie**.

Micky (*turning*) Get away from her.

Maurice *hesitates.*

Jean He's not doing any harm man.

Micky (*beckoning* **Maurice**) Come here.

Maurice *approaches him but stays out of reach.*

I told you to stop running about.

Pause.

Sit down and do your words.

Pause / **Maurice** *looks at him blankly.*

SIT DOWN AND DO YOUR WORDS.

Pause.

Maurice Dead . . . dead.

Maurice *turns and runs towards* **Jeannie**, *opening his overcoat to show off his football shirt as in Act Two.*

Maurice (*to* **Jeannie**) Mira . . . Gazza . . . Mira . . . Gazza . . . Mira . . . Gazza.

Stands looking at **Jeannie**, *holding his coat open.*

Jean (*upset*) Jesus Christ.

Maurice *goes and kneels by the settee, his head resting against* **Jeannie**'s *body, whimpering to himself.*

Micky Come away man, for Christ's sake.

Jean What's the matter, frightened he's showing you up?

Micky How in fuck's name is *he* showing *me* up? Huh?

Jean At least he's got feelings. You . . .

Micky And I haven't, is that what . . .

Jean You might have, only you don't let anyone . . .

Micky Cos that's the way I am, right?

*Pause / **Micky** turns to face downstage.*

Best way.

*Long pause, during which upstage lights fade down, leaving **Maurice** and **Jeannie** in half light.*

Jean When was the last time you cried?

Pause.

When was the last time you cried about anything? Huh?

Pause.

When you were seven year old was it?

Pause.

Micky Fucked if I know.

Jean Oh but I reckon you do. Seven year old was it?

Pause.

When she left you in the Assistance?

Micky (*turning, angry*) She didn't leave *me* in the Assistance, she left *him* in the Assistance. Right?

Pause.

Got it?

Jean Oh I've got it all right. Same as what you told that teacher. How she left *him* in the Assistance cos she couldn't cope. How they came and took *you* as well, just to make up the set. Like playing rummy, only with kids. Which is why you don't trust them. Which is why you don't send for them, even when your mother is coughing up her last.

Pause.

Micky (*turning to face downstage*) That's about the size of it.

Jean Only I know different.

Micky (*quietly*) Yeah?

Jean It was last week she told me about it. After you'd had that row with the social workers, about her going into a home.

Micky (*turning angrily*) It was *her* didn't want to go into a home, nowt to do with . . .

Jean (*interrupting*) Bother to ask her did you? Or did you make her mind up *for* her, same as you always do?

Pause / he turns back to face downstage.

I *know* she didn't want to be put away, she wasn't friggin daft.

Pause.

But she wanted to tell them herself. Not have you butting in, doing it for her. Like she was nowt. Well, she's nowt now I suppose, so you can please yourself what . . .

Micky (*interrupting, turning angrily*) Look, I didn't want her put in a home, right?

Jean Why not? It was what she did to you wasn't it?

Pause / he turns to face downstage.

Good as anyway, leaving you in the Assistance. She must have known . . .

Micky (*interrupting, turning angrily*) She didn't leave *me* in the Assistance, right?

Jean Oh no, of course she didn't. Just like she's not friggin dead. Just like every time you're in court. And where were you Mr Robson on the night in question? Oh I was a hundred miles away your honour with my feet up, watching the tele. Along with six other people. And here's their statements to prove it. Just like that. Magic. Magic friggin daddy. And you get so you believe it. You even believe it yourself.

Pause / he turns to face downstage.

Can't say I blame you mind. Must be a hard thing to take, when you're seven year old, that mammy doesn't want you. Bit of a shaker was it?

Micky *starts to turn, stops, faces back downstage.*

Bit of a shaker all right. I mean, you were daddy's little man weren't you? Just like Michael is now. Till daddy pissed off.

Micky (*quietly*) He didn't piss off.

Jean What?

Micky He didn't piss off, he got sent down.

Jean Oh that's right, he got sent down. And then he sort of forgot to come back, was that it?

Pause.

Well, she said he pissed off, but she might have got it wrong. We'll need to check that out with her when she comes round, huh?

Pause / Jean looks over at Jeannie.

Any minute now I reckon.

Pause.

Well he was away anyhow. And her left with two bairns, and nowt to put in their mouths cos the Assistance wouldn't give her anything. Investigating her claim, or summat daft.

Pause.

And you know what one of them said to her? 'Money, Mrs Robson? Well, we'll have to see about that. Only don't hold your breath. Could take quite a time to sort out. I mean, you've never worked have you? Apart from laying on your back that is.'

Gets up, stands down right, facing downstage.

She needed money desperate. Could have got somebody to mind the bairns and gone down Elswick Road, that would have been easy. But she wanted to get back at them. Especially for saying that.

Pause / she looks across at him, then turns to face downstage again.

So she hits on an idea. The Assistance won't give her any money for the bairns, so let the Assistance look after them. But don't do it nice and quiet, so nobody notices. Pick a time when the place is jam packed with half the West End of Newcastle, all sweating on whether they're going to get owt or nowt for the weekend. Owt or nowt. Pick a Friday afternoon, after the bars have shut.

Pause / she looks across at him.

But here's a thing. She's got two bairns. One of them's a right worky, especially now the father's not around to check him.

Pause / she continues looking at him for a moment, then turns to face downstage again.

But there's another one. Four year old. Never says nowt. A bit backward. Just sits on the table and grins all the time. Lets the lasses dress him up and cart him round the streets in a pram. Has to be spoon fed. Never says a word.

Pauses, then looking at him.

So what does she do? Leave both of them? Hardly. She did that, they'd be so busy stopping the one from setting fire to the place they'd never notice the other one was there. Bit of a puzzler then. Must have taken her days to work it out. Which one does she leave, the one who'll scream the place down or the one who'll sit there grinning? The worky or the dummy? Mad Micky or mental Maurice?

Pause / he looks at her.

Remember that, do you, when she left you on the counter in the Assistance? The time you screamed the place down? The last time you cried?

Pause / he turns to face her.

Micky (*pointing at* **Jeannie**) She . . . she told me different.

Jean Different.

Micky She always said it was Maurice got left.

Jean Oh, *she* said it was Maurice got left, is that it? And you believed her. Just like that. Magic.

Pause.

Well I mean, it's not the sort of thing you'd remember *yourself*, is it? Seven year old and yer mam leaves you screaming in the Assistance. Happens every day. Soon forgotten about, like one of them football scores. Newcastle two, Sunderland one.

Maurice (*still kneeling, voice subdued*) Mira . . . Gazza.

Jean (*advancing slowly towards* **Micky**) Know why she told you different? She was frightened of you. Even as a bairn. So she told you they'd come for you second, just to make up the set. And it suited you, made you feel hard done by. Not by her, by them. Them vultures flying over. I mean, couldn't blame *mammy* could you? Bit too close to home that, like breaking in and

.smashing up your own front room. Your home in the West, gone. I mean, it couldn't have been *her little man* that mammy dumped, could it? It must have been the other one. I mean, you can tell *him* owt, can't you, it works like magic. He'll swallow anything, will *mental Maurice*.

Pause / she stops a couple of paces from him.

Micky (*with no force*) I'll have you Jean.

Jean (*leaning towards him*) Yes?

Pause.

Like fuck.

They stare at each other, then he looks away, downstage.

Know what else? She reckoned you knew all along, knew it was you that got left. Only you didn't let on, and she didn't, like it was a secret between the two of you, something no one else knew about. And you never let on, not even to each other. But you knew all right. DIDN'T YOU?

Long pause / he continues to look downstage.

And here's the best part. The second piece of magic. The first piece was only clever. This piece is *dead fucking clever*. And what's best about it is you worked it all out yourself. At seven year old. Cos no one likes being *dumped* do they Micky?

Pause.

So, first piece of magic: pretend it never happened. And the second piece of magic: *make sure it never happens again*. By making yourself perfect, so no one can touch you, not even . . . (*Touching him with her finger.*) . . . lay a finger on you. The hardest. The best dressed. Not frightened of anything. The cock that'll have women all over Newcastle crawling on their hands and knees, just to get a taste of it. Crawling over all the other men. To get to you.

*Upstage lights slowly fade up to full. Whilst this is happening, **Jean** takes hold of **Micky** and turns him to face towards **Jeannie**.*

Well it's worked. You're fucking perfect. Nothing can get to you. We need cash, we'll get it ourselves. We fall sick, we'll get ourselves well. Don't call us, we'll call you. Only we won't.

Micky (*pushing her away, not violently*) Get away.

Jean *looks at him, then goes and sits at the right end of the settee, next to* **Jeannie**'s *head.*

Jean (*touching the blanket*) Ho'way man Jeannie, don't you want to see how your little man's turned out? You've done a fine job, the pair of you.

Pause.

A fine job, eh Micky?

Long pause.

Micky DON'T TOUCH ME. LEAVE ME ALONE.

Long pause / they stare at each other.

Jean (*quietly*) Leave you alone? (*Speaks as if to a child.*) No, that's not what you want. (*Slowly unbuttons her blouse, takes out one breast.*) Is this it?

Pause.

Is this what you want Micky?

Long pause, then he takes a step towards her. She slowly shakes her head. He stops. She looks down, then at him, puts her breast away. Then speaks, normal voice.

Cold.

Long pause / they stare at each other. Then **Jean** *looks down at* **Jeannie**, *touches the blanket.*

Jean Want to . . .

Micky (*turning away*) Na.

Maurice (*mechanically*) Na, na, na. Na, na, na.

Jean (*touching his shoulder*) All right man. (*Starts rebuttoning her blouse.*) We'd best get her back.

Pause.

Micky?

Micky *half turns.*

We'd best get her back. Home.

Pause.

We'd best get her back home man.

Micky (*turning back downstage*)   I'm not touching her.

Long pause.

Jean SHARON!

*Pause, then **Sharon** opens the door of bedroom one. She is wearing a nightdress, dressing gown, and slippers. She has been crying.*

Come and give us a hand man. We've got to take Jeannie back. She's . . .

Sharon (*upset*)   Aye, I know.

Sharon *takes hold of* **Jeannie**'s *legs while* **Jean** *takes her upper body.* **Micky** *remains facing downstage.*

Jean (*moving **Maurice** gently out of the way*)   Ho'way man.

Jean *and* **Sharon** *move* **Jeannie** *off the settee.* **Maurice** *scrambles up and hovers anxiously.*

Jean Micky.

Pause / no reaction.

You'll have to drive the car man.

Micky Aye.

They take **Jeannie** *towards the door,* **Maurice** *hovering behind them. They pause at the door,* **Jean** *looks back at* **Micky**.

Jean Ho'way.

Jean *and* **Sharon** *exit with* **Jeannie**. *Sound of descending.* **Maurice** *is torn between following them and staying with* **Micky**. *Pause.*

Maurice MRNDNAA!

Pause.

ARGNTNAA!

Micky *turns, looks at* **Maurice**, *walks slowly towards the door. Once* **Maurice** *has seen him coming, he exits downstairs after the others.* **Micky** *exits. Sound of descending. Sound of car doors etc.*

Sharon (*off*)   Get off man.

Sound of **Sharon** *ascending. Sound of car driving away.* **Sharon** *enters, comes to sit at left end of the settee, stares straight ahead. Sound of* **Sean** *getting up, painfully. Sound of* **Sean** *ascending, slowly.*

Sean (*singing, off*)

> Who's gonna hold you little darling
> Who's gonna hold you to their breast
> Who's gonna talk your future over
> While I'm ramblin' in the West.

(*Shouts.*) Hey, Sharon. You there Sharon?

Sean *enters, stands in the doorway, looking at her.*

Sean Hey, Sharon.

Sharon *continues to stare ahead.*

Lights fade slowly to black.

Act Four

In the darkness, the sound of a guitar. Then lights fade up to reveal set as at the end of Act Three. The clock now shows half past one. **Sharon** *is sitting as before, at the left end of the settee.* **Sean** *is sitting in the armchair, gently strumming his guitar. During this Act the light should be mainly focused on the downstage area, giving it a red glow as if from firelight. The remainder of the set (i.e. all the upstage area behind the settee) should be dimly lit.*

Sean How's this. (*Sings.*)

As I walked out on a bright May morning
Through the busy streets of the shining town
I came to a gently flowing river
And by its banks I lay me down

Come in come in, said the river to me
Come in young man and taste my waters deep
Oh I have ways to ease the pain that haunts you
And in my arms you'll surely sleep

But the water was cold and the month November
And the icy current dragged me down
And I heard the river laughing at me
It seems young man you'll surely drown

I woke up cold by the flowing river
And I turned my steps to the empty town
And I was a drowned man, drowned man walking
My heart like water running down

Pause.

Well?

Sharon All right.

Sean How all right?

Sharon Just all right.

Sean I mean, did you like the words?

Sharon The tune was all right.

Sean Christ man I didn't write the bleedin tune.

Pause.

I mean, it's not a song for the club or owt like that.

Sharon Why not?

Sean I don't think they'd take to the words.

Sharon That's what I said. The tune's all right though.

*Pause / **Sean** starts strumming gently.*

Sean No, I reckon I've got to start looking for a different sort of audience.

Sharon Where, like?

Pause.

See the teacher did you?

Sean Aye.

Sharon Fancy her, did you?

Sean *stops strumming.*

Sean Well now. There's a question. She was an intelligent woman. I could see that all right.

Sharon I'm asking did you fancy her.

Sean Well now. I'd say she was an intelligent woman, and not exactly a bad looking woman. And I'd say she had a fine sense of clothes. But no, I didn't.

Sharon You didn't fancy her?

Sean Christ man, I'm not the sort of bloke that fancies everything wearing a skirt.

Sharon Some lads do.

Sean Ah well, that's it you see. Some lads. Sean Grogan is Sean Grogan. Which is not the same as being some lads. It's like the races. Some fellers will go through the whole card, fling all their money away in the first five minutes. Meantime Sean's in the paddock, casting his eye over the field for the first race. And if he doesn't see anything he fancies, his money stays in his pocket. But when something really does catch his eye – and it might not be till the third or the fourth – *then* he'll place his bet. He's committed. And the horse knows it. The horse is committed. The horse is committed, and Sean is committed.

Sharon And does the horse win?

Sean   More often than not, no. But that's not the point. It's not the winning, it's the knowing.

He starts to strum the guitar.

Sharon   I thought you might have done.

Sean   What.

Sharon   Fancied her.

Sean   Christ man, you want to try singing a different tune.

Sharon   I told you, the tune's all right, it's the words that need changing.

*They laugh / **Sean** stops strumming.*

You're different from what I thought you'd be. From when you first came up I mean.

Sean   How'd you mean?

Sharon   I don't know. Just different. Perhaps it's me that's different. To what I was when you first came up.

Sean   Aye well, two years is a long time in a young girl's life. But when you get to my age, two years is just . . . (*Strums two chords.*) . . . two years.

Sharon   You're not that old.

Sean   I'm twenty-eight.

Sharon   You're younger than mam.

Sean   (*drawling, playing cowboy chords*)   Well that's just one of them things I guess.

They laugh.

How'd you mean, different?

Sharon   Perhaps it's me like I said.

Pause.

Sean   Aye well. All it used to be with me was back that horse, drink that pint. Then it was shift that muck, back that horse, drink that pint. And now it's shift that muck, back that horse, drink that pint, strum this guitar. My world's getting bigger all the time.

Sharon   So where does mam fit in?

Sean Jean?

Sharon You never mentioned her. It should be 'something' that Jean.

Sean You mean . . .

Both Shift that muck, back that horse, drink that pint, strum this guitar, 'something' . . . that Jean.

Sharon Aye.

Pause / **Sean** *starts strumming.*

Sean Well it's funny but I can't seem to think of that something, and me being a regular poet and all.

Sean *continues to gently strum the guitar. Then, sound of car approaching and pulling up outside. One car door opens, then slams. After a few seconds, sound of* **Jean** *coming upstairs.* **Jean** *enters, comes forward into the light.*

Jean What happened to the light?

Sharon Bulb's gone.

Jean Well why didn't you put another one in?

Sharon Couldn't find one in the dark.

Jean You want to stop being so cheeky. (*To* **Sean**.) And you'd have been better to have spent your time fixing the front door instead of plonking about on that thing. That guitar's not going to stop them breaking in.

Sean And that door's not going to get me to the Palladium.

Jean *sits down at the right end of the settee.*

Jean I can see I'm going to have to get on to the council to get it fixed.

Pause / **Sean** *stops strumming.*

Sean How are you Sean? Nice to see you up and about again. Did you hurt yourself falling downstairs? Well I'm not too bad thanks. Could have been worse. Bit of a headache, a few bruises. Nice of you to ask though.

Jean Well that's all right then. (*To* **Sharon**.) What are you still doing up?

Sharon Nowt.

Jean Nowt. Everything's nowt round here.

Sharon How'd you mean, like?

Jean (*to* **Sean**) Got any tabs?

Sean *shakes his head.*

Jean (*to* **Sharon**) You see? Nowt. (*To* **Sean**.) Any brown ale left?

Sean *shakes his head.*

Jean (*to* **Sharon**) You see? Nowt. Now. What are you still doing up?

Sharon Nowt.

Jean You see? Even the light bulb's nowt. Might as well smash the whole place up and start again.

Pause.

Sharon What's happened to Jeannie?

Jean How should I know I'm not God Sharon.

Pause.

They've taken her away. Maurice wanted to go with her.

Pause.

Sean Did you mean that?

Jean What.

Sean Smash the whole place up and start again.

Jean It wouldn't take much smashing up. Eight pounds worth of damage I reckon.

Sean No, start again.

Jean Look, it's too late for riddles man.

Sean What's here for us? You said it yourself. Nowt.

Jean In this house you mean?

Sean Not just in this house. Up here. It's all nowt, just like you said. First words when you get back: have you fixed the front door cos they'll be breaking in.

Jean Well where else is there?

Sean London.

Jean London.

Sean Aye, London.

Jean Know what it's like down there do you? Been there have you?

Sean Aye, a couple of times.

Jean A couple of times.

Sean Look Jean, I know folks down there. Irish lads. It's like little Ireland down there. Plenty of work, no problem getting a start. And there'd be lots of folk willing to put us up till we got ourselves sorted out. Plenty of singing in the pubs. I might even be able to go full time with the singing.

Jean What about Sharon?

Sean She'd come with us.

Jean She's still at school man.

Sean There's schools down there. And anyway, she's only got another six months. I could go down first, find somewhere for the three of us. In the spring, when the work is picking up. By the time that's been done, she'll be all but finished anyway with the schooling. It wouldn't hurt for her to miss the last few weeks.

Jean I'm not having her missing any school, I've got enough trouble with Michael.

Sharon I wouldn't mind.

Pause.

Jean How come there's suddenly only three of us?

Sean I'm not taking bleedin Micky.

Jean Not Micky. Michael.

Pause.

Sean Sharon said they might be taking him away.

Jean (*to* **Sharon**) Oh you did, did you? First I heard about it.

Pause / **Sharon** *makes a face at* **Sean**.

First I heard about it.

Pause.

Well?

Sean He might be all right, Michael. He might be all right. If they don't take him away I mean. Once he's away from Micky, he might be all right.

Jean How's that like?

Sean You said it yourself, it's Micky keeps stirring him up.

Jean Aye well.

Pause.

Sean For Christ sake Jean, I'm giving us all a chance.

Jean Giving yourself a chance more like.

Sean It's a chance for all of us.

Pause.

Jean How about Micky seeing the bairn.

Sean How'd you mean.

Jean If we went, how would Micky go on about seeing the bairn?

Sean That's his problem.

Jean It wouldn't be right to stop him seeing the bairn if he wanted.

Pause.

I'd have to talk it over with him.

Sean Who?

Jean Micky.

Sean You'd have to talk it over with Micky? When was the last time anybody talked anything over with Micky?

Jean I've been talking to him tonight.

Sean Aye, so I've heard.

Jean Seems like you've been hearing a lot of things while I've been out.

*Pause / **Sean** shrugs.*

Anyway.

Sean Anyway what.

Jean Anyway I'll talk it over with Micky.

Sean And what if he says no?

Pause.

What if he says no?

Jean If he says no he says no, that's all.

Sean And where does that leave us?

Pause.

And where does that leave us, huh?

Pause / **Sean** *gets up, starts walking around.*

Look. It's me, Sean, asking you, Jean, and her, Sharon, to come to London. And maybe Michael. I don't see what it's got to do with anyone else.

Jean Well you wouldn't would you.

Pause.

You want to take a tumble to yourself. There's not just you in the world.

Pause.

I'll have to talk to Micky about it, that's all I'm saying.

Sean You're talking about somebody that's just now nearly killed us.

Jean That was your own fault.

Pause.

Sean So you've been talking to him tonight.

Jean Aye.

Sean And how was he. Tonight. When you were talking to him.

Jean He was upset.

Sean Upset.

Jean Christ man his mother had just friggin died.

Pause.

Sharon He didn't look like he was upset to me.

Jean You keep your nose out.

Pause.

He don't get upset like other people.

Sean He doesn't do anything like other people.

Pause.

Jean It wasn't Jeannie, it was me that upset him.

Sean You upset him.

Jean First time ever. First time I've been able to get right up to him. First time . . . first time I've ever seen him frightened.

Sean Frightened of what?

Pause.

Frightened of what?

Long pause.

Jean It always felt like I'd got a fist inside of us. In my throat, letting nothing in. Just a fist, all the time hardening. Everything I said had to squeeze out past it. And I thought, one day I'm going to wake up and that's all there'll be of me, a fist.

Pause.

But then tonight when I was talking to Micky, something happened. The fist came out. It felt so good at the time, using that fist. I'd waited long enough. But then after, it wouldn't fit back in my throat. The fist wouldn't close back up. And then I thought, well, nowt to bother. What can you catch hold of with a fist?

Pause.

I want to catch hold of Micky. Before it closes back up.

Pause.

If you'd asked me before about going to London I'd have said yes like a shot.

Pause.

Sean Always that fucking Micky. I should have given him a good hiding when I had the chance.

Sharon You haven't lost it he's still sitting outside.

Sean What'd you mean?

Sharon The car's never driven away.

Sean *goes to the window, peers out round the curtain.*

Jean Well?

Sean He's still there all right.

Jean What's he doing?

Sean Just sitting there. There's someone in the back.

Jean Maurice.

Sean *continues to look out the window.*

Come away man.

Sean *puts back the curtain, returns to sit in the armchair.*

Sean He's like a fuckin stone in your shoe that bloke, a stone in your shoe that's working its way into your skin.

Jean Into your bone more like.

*Pause / **Sean** starts strumming the guitar, more violently than before.*

Sean Well I'm going to get the bastard out if you're not.

Pause / he stops strumming.

What's he doing out there?

Jean How the fuck should I know?

Sean WHAT'S HE DOING OUT THERE?

Jean WHY DON'T YOU GO AND ASK HIM SEAN?

Pause.

Sean Why's he sitting out there Jean?

Jean Cos he's got nowhere to go.

Sean What?

Jean BECAUSE. HE'S. GOT. NOWHERE. ELSE. TO. FRIGGIN. GO. All right?

Sean *stares at* **Jean**, *then begins to strum the guitar, more gently this time.*

Sharon   Mam.

Jean   What.

Sharon   Is it all right if I sleep with you tonight?

Jean   Aye I suppose so.

Pause.

Jean (*to* **Sean**)   You sleep with Michael, all right?

Pause.

We're going to bed. Come on Sharon.

Sharon *and* **Jean** *get up, go towards bedroom two.* **Sharon** *exits.* **Sean** *stops strumming.*

Sean   Jean.

Jean (*at the bedroom door*)   What.

Sean   I've made up my mind. To go to London. I'll send you the address up when I've found us a place.

Jean   Aye.

Jean *exits to bedroom two.* **Sean** *strums the guitar, then slowly plays the tune only (just one verse) of 'Drowned Man Walking'. Suddenly throws the guitar down, goes over to the window, throws open the curtains, opens the window.*

Sean (*shouting out of the window*)   It's all right. You've got somewhere to go now. You can move in here. But she's probably told you that already has she? You'll be all right now. Back to your mammy's breasts. To your mammy's breasts, do you hear?

Pause, then car starts up. Sound of it reversing violently. The headlights shine through the window. Then it starts forward at high speed. The headlights track across the room, then disappear. **Sean** *runs from the window. There is a crash, and sound of falling masonry. Simultaneous blackout.*